GULF WAR

A COMPREHENSIVE GUIDE TO PEOPLE, PLACES & WEAPONS

COL. WALTER J. BOYNE,
U.S.A.F. (RET.)

Walter J. Boyne is a retired colonel from the United States Air Force and a prominent military consultant and writer. He has flown over 5000 hours in a score of different aircraft, from a Piper Cub to a B-1B, and is a Command Pilot. Col. Boyne is former director of the National Air and Space Museum and is the best-selling author of *The Smithsonian Book of Flight*, *The Leading Edge*, and the forthcoming novel, *Eagles At War*.

Special acknowledgement to Dr. Ibrahim Oweiss, Department of Economics, Intercultural Center, Georgetown University, for his consultation.

CONTENTS

The Middle East: A History of Conflict

In 1939, Winston Churchill said that Russia was "a riddle wrapped in a mystery inside an enigma." It might similarly be said that the Middle East is disunity, multiplied by wealth and many people, divided by divergent beliefs and opposing political aims . . . yet united by Islam and by the Arabic language. This vast land area, with its enormous oil reserves, has since the beginning of time been the seat of wars and strife, just as it has been the seat of civilization and the progenitor of many great cultures. It combines religious fervor with savage brutality, endless avarice with incomparable giving, the warrior's code with inexplicable treachery, and Pan-Arab goals with individual gain.

Wars have raged continuously across the region, from Crusaders and Saracens battling with sword and scimitar, through the romantic-looking but deadly Bedouin engagements, to the dervish-against-Red Coat battles that look so handsome on the movie screen and were so desperately fought on the region's deserts. Later, two great world wars swirled across those same endless sands. From 1914 to 1918 huge armies were squandered in battles now crowded from memory by the slaughter on Europe's Western Front. Dimly remembered images remain of Rolls-Royce armored cars, and primitive camel caravans intersecting with Model T trucks, but the true battles were fought day by day, in the heat and the thirst, by infantry dug into sand trenches. The Allied cause was greatly aided by a widespread Arab revolt, aided by Lawrence of Arabia, against the Turkish remnants of the dying Ottoman empire.

The tradition of combat—exemplified here by Crusaders battling Saracens—is long-established in the Middle East.

In World War II almost the first good news the British had was their astounding defeat, against overwhelming odds, of the Italian armies opposing them. Then Germany stiffened Italian resistance with the famous Afrika Korps, a scratch unit commanded by a man even the British could admire openly, General (later Field Marshal) Erwin Rommel. In a world desperate for some sense of cheer, the battles of the Afrika Korps against the British Eighth Army "Desert Rats" seemed to add a soccer game quality to the war as first one side and then the other won break-through battles and dashed across the North African sands. It was not soccer, of course—it was hard and bitter fighting.

World War II was far from the end of Middle East violence. As the exhausted foreign powers withdrew, unable to withstand the swelling tides of Arab nationalism, the region echoed throughout the 1960s, '70s, and '80s with ever more vicious conflicts like the Arab-Israeli wars, the disintegration of Lebanon, and the ghastly eight-year struggle between Iraq and Iran.

Reasons for war

The causes of war in the Middle East have varied. Some of the conflicts erupted over religion, territory, tribal feuds, and trade routes, but greed was always the underlying common denominator, epitomized by the lust for oil that has characterized so much of recent world history.

If the Middle East is to be truly understood by a Westerner—and few Westerners do understand—a number of things must be accepted. Above all is the fundamental nature of Islam, which will be discussed later. Another, almost equally important factor is the often shifting hierarchy of loyalties that most Arabs feel. Of these, the most intense, immediate loyalty is to the family—father and mother, unmarried daughters and the sons and their families. (This blood-loyalty has been demonstrated time and again in both the shifts of power—often by assassination, usually by revolution—which occur within the Arab nations, and in the almost immediate recoalescence of power in a new family.) Next, in descending order, comes

Oil, symbolized by this refinery at Ahmadi, Kuwait, has been both the curse and salvation of the Middle East.

Morning prayer—practiced here by a Kuwaiti delegation to Saudi Arabia—is just one element of Islamic duty.

loyalty to the tribe, to the region, to the particular religious sect within Islam, and finally to the state. Concurrent with these loyalties, and sometimes overlapping them, is the concept of loyalty to Arabism and Islam as a whole, particularly in concert with assistance to developing Muslim countries.

The existence of these multiple loyalties has prevented many Middle Eastern countries from creating strong political parties based on philosophy rather than on personalities. And these same multiple loyalties are reflected in the changing national alliances that have been so infinitely varied and complex over the years. The Arab nations sometimes have joined together in a political union, as Egypt and Syria did from 1958 to 1961 and as was proposed by Egypt and Libya in 1972 and Syria and Iraq in 1979. Yet in the shifting political sands of the Middle East, it is not uncommon for countries at one moment so bound in brotherhood that they wish to unite to be unofficially at war a few months later.

The Gulf crisis that began to take tangible form in the summer of 1990 offers two outstanding examples of the flexibility of Arab allegiances. The first is Syria's joining in the coalition with its bitterly denounced enemy, the United States, against its one-time political brother, Iraq; the second is Iran's tacit, if limited, support of Iraq after eight years of the most vicious war in Middle East history.

These complex situations, interrelated at personal, party, and national levels, require intensive study even to begin to comprehend. In addition, there are in the equation other important elements that are obvious and understandable. The first is Arab resentment against the colonial powers—Italy, France, and especially Great Britain in the glory days of its empire—a resentment transferred in later years to the United States. The anger stems from a number of sources, but the most important one is the ruthless exploitation of Middle Eastern oil by the West.

The second easily grasped element of the Middle East equation is the implacable Arab hatred of Israel, victor not only in five cruel wars but also of the peace that followed four of them. And because the United States has been Israel's loyal ally, its political and military enforcer, that Arab frustration extends to it as well. Furthermore, the United States' apparent disinterest in the Palestinian quest for self-determination has had a negative impact on the feelings of the Arabs.

The impact of Islam

As historically important as religion has been in the West (think of the Crusades, the Thirty Years War, the Inquisition, the "conversion" of the New World), Christianity has never had the impact upon its members that Islam has had on the nations and the peoples of the Middle East. There, it is not just a

*The Shiite Moslem feast of Ashoura inspires this
believer in Lebanon to strike his head with a
sword. For many Muslims, devotion to God is
total.*

religion but a way of life. The word Islam means
"peace," which also implies total submission to God.
Islam extends beyond ordinary religious concepts
into every aspect of lay existence, and is as much a
legal code as a religious one.

The third monotheistic (one-God) religion to
emerge in the region, after Judaism and Christianity,
Islam was propagated by the Prophet Muhammad in
Arabia during the seventh century. The Muslims
who profess the Islamic religion see it as an exten-
sion—and correction—of Judaism and Christianity.

The basic theological principles are simple—the profession of faith that "there is no god but one God and Muhammad is his Prophet" and a complete submission to the will of God. Supporting this simple profession are the five basic duties of every true believer—the "pillars of Islam." These include 1.) the "Shahada" or testimony—the profession of faith; 2.) the performance of the "Salat" or formal prayer, five times a day; 3.) "Zakat" or the giving of alms to the poor; 4.) fasting during the month of Ramadan, the eighth month of the Moslem year; and 5.) "Hajj," a pilgrimage to Mecca made once in the lifetime of all capable of doing so. Unfortunately, there looms a sixth pillar, one that all of the Allied planners of Desert Storm were forced to consider, that of "Jihad"—the holy war to defend the faith. A brave enemy soldier is one thing; a brave enemy soldier convinced that his death will be a martyrdom rewarded in Paradise is quite another. Especially disconcerting to the Western mind is the Islamic assertion that terrorists are part of the Jihad: the assassin as martyr.

Differing factions, differing beliefs

Although there are many Islamic sects, two major branches compose almost 90 percent of the world's Moslems. The first is the Shi'a, whose followers are Shi'ites; the second is the Sunni, which in the past controlled almost every government in the Islamic world. The Shi'ites are fundamentalists, whose belief that further interpretation of Islamic doctrine is possible has led to innumerable, and often fanatical, subgroups. The Sunnis tend to restrict interpretation and as a result have a more cohesive structure.

These political/philosophic divisions are most important in terms of the Gulf crisis and its potential expansion. The fundamentalists' surge to power was led by the late Ayatollah Khomeini, who as the leader of the Shi'ites stressed Islamic populism and called for a Pan-Arab return to the basic tenets of Islam. Opposing the fundamentalists are the more modern states, whose allegiance to Islam is not less, but whose awareness of the requirements of coexistence in the real, modern world is perhaps greater. Of greatest pertinence to the Gulf war is the fact that Iraqi leader Saddam Hussein now portrays his invasion of Iran and the eight years of bloody war that followed as the self-sacrificing containment of the Ayatollah Khomeini, a manning of the ramparts of the emerging Arab world against crazed fundamentalists. And Saddam is respected by many Arabs for this as well as for his uncompromising opposition to Israel. (Ironically, most of Iraq's army were Shi'ite soldiers led by Sunni officers.)

Development of Islam

Islam has grown in battle over the centuries. The Prophet Muhammad was born at Mecca in the year 570 A.D.; 59 years later he would conquer that city by force of arms and convert it to the religion he espoused—a trial by sword method still advocated by many Muslims.

There followed uninterrupted centuries of conquest and civil war that saw the influence of Islam spread westward across North Africa into Spain, and eastward beyond Turkey and the fringes of China, into Southeast Asia. (Indonesia is today the largest Muslim country in the world, with more than 120 million Moslems.) The three Muslim empires were larger than that of the Romans, and in many ways, for different periods of time, equally well administered. Inevitably beset over time by internal strife, the Muslim world was able to withstand both Christian crusaders and Mongol invaders, with the last Muslim empire, the Ottoman, lasting until 1922.

Western involvement

Western interest in the Middle East has centered upon trade routes, strategic locations, and, most particularly, petroleum. England clashed with France over Egypt, and with Russia over Persia (Iran). But by the end of the First World War in 1917, England's position as a world power was so great that she virtually dictated events in the Middle East. In concert with the League of Nations, England and France evolved a system of mandates that extended protection to "independent governments" in return for enormous economic and political concessions. It was international puppetry on a grand scale, yet was relatively inexpensive for the great European powers to administer.

The Second World War created the framework for the modern Middle East. As the Allies were presumably fighting for democracy and self-determination, the concept of Arab nationalism was fostered immeasurably. While bitter battles raged all the way from Casablanca to Iraq, and an uneasy truce boiled in Iran, it became apparent that Western influence was weakening even as Arab strength was rising.

A Jewish homeland

But the wars that have torn the area since 1947 can be traced back to 1917 and the Balfour Declara-

Zionist leader Chaim Weizmann was instrumental in the post-World War II creation of a Jewish state in the Middle East. He served from 1949 to 1952 as Israel's first president.

tion, by which the British government indicated that it favored the establishment of a national home for Jewish people in Palestine. Chaim Weizmann, the leader of the Zionists, used the Balfour Declaration to prepare for the formation of a Jewish state by encouraging immigration, which by 1948 had totaled more than half a million people.

Inflamed by the horror of the Holocaust and trained by the war, the Zionists undertook an aggressive campaign to secure a homeland. In the process Britain saw its control of the region slipping away, and appealed to the United Nations for assistance. On November 29, 1947, the General Assembly resolved to partition Palestine to establish a Jewish state and an Arab state within the territory.

The Haganah—the Jewish underground army—secured Israel as a state "born in battle" by defeating the Arab Legion from Transjordan, and the armies of Iraq, Syria, and Egypt after Israel was proclaimed independent on May 14, 1948. As a result of the fighting, many Palestinians were driven out of their homeland, fleeing to Jordan, Syria, and Lebanon, thereby setting the stage for new wars and the creation of the Palestine Liberation Organization.

The humiliation of defeat of these newly created national armies by the army of Israel created an attitude in the Arab world that has steadily worsened over the years. It was abominable to them that Israel had been created, that Palestine had been divided, that Palestinians were refugees from their own country. Israel—to many Arab minds a tiny upstart of a country with less than two million people, with a ragtag army and Piper Cub air force—could defeat the combined Arab forces only because of the support of the United States. There could never be peace—there would always be new wars.

Nasser, Sadat, and continued strife

Israel's population was swollen by massive immigration in the 1950s, but the fledgling nation was threatened on four borders. A tiny country, 250 miles long on the Syrian-Jordan frontier but only ten miles wide at its narrowest point, Israel launched the Sinai war in 1956 to stifle growing Egyptian power, and to secure land as a buffer area against invasion. The Egyptian leader, Jamal Abdel-Nasser, had nationalized the Suez Canal, an action regarded by both Great Britain and France as a threat to world peace. In response, Israel invaded the Sinai and headed for the Canal while France and England opted to "intervene to restore peace" and, incidentally, secure control of the Canal. Israel managed an overwhelming triumph against superior Egyptian forces, only to have the English-French attack against Egypt be aborted by American pressure on its allies.

Incredibly, Nasser emerged from the defeat still a hero to the Arab world, primarily because his loss to

A convoy of Israeli half-tracks passes wrecked Egyptian military vehicles in the Gaza Strip, 1956.

Israel was overshadowed by his almost inadvertent success against France and England. He began a long and bellicose war of words as he rebuilt his strength for another attack. Israel responded with the brilliant "Six Day War" of 1967, when it wiped out Arab air power on the ground, then successively dealt with the opposing land forces. Six days after the fighting began, having defeated the Egyptian, Syrian, and Jordanian armies, Israel captured the Sinai, the West Bank of the Jordan, the Gaza Strip, and the Golan Heights. It now had defensible frontiers—but no peace.

At the Khartoum summit conference of Arab states in September, 1967, it was formally declared that there could be no recognition of Israel, nor negotiations, nor peace.

Nasser once again survived, involving Israel in a long and painful war of attrition that lasted almost until Nasser's death in 1970. He was succeeded in Egypt by Anwar Sadat, who carefully planned the establishment of strong Arab alliances to seek the

The charismatic Egyptian president Jamal Abdel-Nasser galvanized the Arab world for two decades.

recapture of lost territories. Acting in coordination with Syria, he launched an attack on Israel on Yom Kippur, October 6, 1973.

Sadat's carefully planned war opened to outstanding successes all along the front as the highly trained, well-motivated Egyptian troops used Soviet-supplied equipment to enormous advantage. In the East, the Syrians were having a lesser degree of success in attempting to reclaim the Golan Heights. But the Israelis rallied, counter-attacked, and by the 20th of October had succeeded in not only stopping the Egyptian drive, but eliminating their air power so that the powerful Egyptian Third Army was cut off and trapped. Egypt and Israel accepted a cease fire through the United Nations but further fighting resulted in Israel marching all the way to the Gulf of Suez.

Given the conclusion of the 1973 war, in which both Egypt and Israel scored victories, the United States was able to help both sides to achieve a peace agreement under the 1978 Camp David accords.

The 1973 Arab-Israeli war was hard-fought by both sides. Here, Amawein Square in Damascus, Syria, is littered with debris following an Israeli air strike.

The pattern of what by now had become clear Israeli military superiority was continued in Lebanon in 1982, when Israel, concerned about a buildup of Palestinian forces in southern Lebanon, mounted an invasion of the country and drove the Palestinians north all the way to West Beirut, in the center of Lebanon.

The constant series of defeats at the hands of Israel has inflamed much of the Arab world with a sense of unworthiness that it feels can only be overcome by a military victory that would lead to the eradication of Israel and the concomitant humiliation of the United States.

Better weapons, more anger

From the Arab-Israeli wars there emerged a new, and curiously ironic world condition, in which high-technology armament has spread to countries that are, despite their wealth of natural resources, sunk in Third World poverty. Thus the Iran-Iraq military

Iraqi soldiers in occupied Iran pose near a portrait of Iranian leader Ayatollah Khomeini.

conflict of the 1980s saw a combination of the most sophisticated weapons—radars, missiles, and jet planes—and the indiscriminate slaughter of untrained cadres of soldiers, most of whom were no more than boys. In sum, then, the leaders of Iran and Iraq—two countries of immeasurable wealth— chose to squander their resources on endless arrays of modern armament that was left burning in the sand, where the youth of their nations was also squandered, in endlessly destructive ground assaults.

But it was very much the debilitating struggle against Iran, ignobly concluded in a peace agreement that saved face but little else, that caused Iraq's Saddam Hussein to cast his covetous eyes on Kuwait.

Saddam Hussein had a catalog of reasons why Kuwait, and indeed the entire Arab world, "owed him" a great deal. The most important reason, over-shadowing all others, was that Iraq was now the Arab world's deterrent to the most hated enemy, Israel. Then there was Iraq's historic claim to the region, Saddam's view being that the area that is now Kuwait belonged to his Mesopotamian forefathers, and that the current border was only the result of a line drawn in the sand by British overlords—one that left Iraq virtually landlocked. (When the Anglo-Kuwait treaty of 1899 was terminated in 1961, making Kuwait an independent country, the nation was immediately claimed by Iraq, whose claims were frustrated by both England and the Arab League. Iraq tried again in 1973 and 1976.)

Hussein also felt that he had defended Kuwait from the onslaught of Iran's Islamic fundamentalism, and that Iraq's 35 billion dollar war debt should be forgiven. Further, Kuwait had consistently overproduced its OPEC-set oil quotas, lowering the price of oil and reducing income to Iraq at a time when it was most needed. Finally, Hussein accused Kuwait of pumping Iraqi oil from the Rumaila oil field.

George Bush's presidency was put to its toughest test in the summer of 1990, following Iraq's brutal invasion of Kuwait. Iraqi dictator Saddam Hussein had plenty of reasons for his actions, but Bush wasn't buying any of them.

Saddam moves on Kuwait

Hussein sought the discharge of all of these "debts" and the reconstitution of the Iraqi economy, which had been depleted not only by the costs of the Iran war, but by the loss of revenues that resulted from it. The easiest solution was the annexation of Kuwait as Iraq's nineteenth province.

Hussein was certain that the United States would object, but apparently felt that annexation offered a number of overriding advantages. The first of these was his ability to attack Israel at will, and pull the rest of the Arab world into war at his side. The second was his faith in the toughness of his battle-trained troops, and their ability to "hunker down" under U.S. attack and wage a long and bitter land war, as he'd been forced to do against Iran. Finally, he had seen the reaction of the American populace to a long war in Vietnam, and felt that no American administration would have the courage to make what many would call the same mistake again.

And it undoubtedly occurred to Hussein that if he could successfully defy the United States, he would attain a position of leadership in the Arab world comparable to that established by the beloved Nasser. In addition, his possession of approximately 20 percent

Iraqi strongman Saddam Hussein made a colossal miscalculation by assuming that he could annex Kuwait with impunity.

On August 9, 1990, the UN Security Council voted to condemn Iraq. The United States ambassador is Thomas Pickering.

of the world's oil reserves in both Iraq and Kuwait would make his country an economic giant, with the potential of breaking the will not only of traditional enemies like the United States and England but of friends and trading partners like the Soviet Union and Japan. Iraq would be the superpower of the Middle East, and Saddam Hussein *was* Iraq. It was a heady prospect, one that a man of his ruthless nature could not forgo.

While Hussein has rarely miscalculated in internal politics (one safeguard he has against internal miscalculation is a powerful incentive program of death for failure or even the whiff of discord), he has often miscalculated on the international scene. And he did again when he marched into Kuwait.

But the United States had made massive miscalculations, too, the most important of which was the support it had furnished Iraq because it was fighting Iran. A less important, but still crucial, error was the virtual encouragement of Iraq's aggression against

Kuwait by incorrect messages transmitted by American Ambassador April Glaspie to the effect that the United States regarded the Iraq-Kuwait dispute as an intra-Arab matter.

Hussein had clearly telegraphed his intentions by massing forces on the Kuwait border, demanding that Kuwait and the United Arab Emirates stop overproduction of oil, and demanding a rise in price to $25 a barrel.

OPEC settled for a $21 price; to Hussein this was the equivalent of an almost three billion dollar annual loss in foreign exchange revenues. Confident that the United States would back down in the face of a *fait accompli,* Saddam Hussein sent his troops roaring across the Kuwaiti border at two o'clock in the morning of August 2, 1990; they raced up the six-lane highway to Kuwait City, and after sporadic but sharp fighting had secured the entire country by evening. The Emir of Kuwait, Sheik Jabir al-Ahmad al-Sabah, had time to flee to Saudi Arabia.

The world reacted with almost universal condemnation as Saddam announced that he would make Kuwait a graveyard if anyone attempted to stop him, while at the same time denying that he had any intention to invade Saudi Arabia. Saddam set up a provisional government that lasted only five days, at which time Kuwait was formally annexed by Iraq as its nineteenth province. Hostages—"guests" in Iraqi terminology—were seized in Iraq and Kuwait, and it would be long agonizing months before they were finally released.

Desert Shield

The General Assembly of the United Nations voted, without dissent, tough economic sanctions

Downtown Baghdad is illuminated by the January 16, 1991, Allied bombing raid that opened the Gulf War.

against Iraq—sanctions that all UN members were required to obey. It would be the first of a series of resolutions condemning Iraq's actions, culminating with one that authorized the use of force if Iraq had not begun a substantive withdrawal from Kuwait by January 15, 1991.

The United States began a quick and massive military build-up, code-named "Desert Shield," surpassing in speed and scale anything seen during the Vietnamese war. President Bush and Secretary of State James Baker made continual diplomatic efforts to shore up the coalition against Iraq, a coalition made at once strong and fragile by Arab members like Egypt, Syria, and Morocco. While maintaining a firm determination to eject Iraq from Kuwait, the U.S. sought face-to-face talks with Saddam Hussein, and welcomed the efforts of other peacemakers, including President Francois Mitterrand of France, King Hussein of Jordan, and the Secretary General of the United Nations, Javier Perez de Cuellar. President Bush spoke firmly about the UN objectives while calling for peace. At the same time, he deftly worked with the U.S. Congress to obtain approval for undertaking the fulfillment of the United Nations resolution.

Would-be peacemakers ranging from American political figure Jesse Jackson to PLO leader Yasser Arafat snatched an extra 15 minutes of fame on a world stage. In the meantime, Saddam Hussein became more and more bellicose, demanding that the invasion of Kuwait be linked to the Palestinian question. Through it all the world looked on with disbelief; to many historians the situation seemed reminiscent of the last, gloomy days of July 1914 or of August 1939, as despite all of the efforts to find a solution, war became inevitable.

Iraq had lost more than 120,000 men and spent more than 120 billion dollars in the war against Iran. Iraq has the climate, the location, and the population to be the richest and most prosperous nation in the Middle East. Yet Iraq had determined that it would not give up Kuwait. The United States had determined, in concert with almost all of the nations of the world, that Iraq would.

Desert Storm unleashed

The test of wills to determine which country would prevail—Iraq or the United States—came to a head on January 16, 1991, when Desert Shield became Desert Storm, and United Nations forces launched an all-out air attack against Iraqi positions. War had come once again to the troubled Middle East.

The troubled Middle East.

The World, the Modern Military, and War in the Gulf

The United States operates at a terrific disadvantage in any relation with Arab states because it has no idea of the depth and breadth of hatred that much of the Arab population feels for it. The degree of the hatred felt—and increasingly expressed—by the anti-American faction is appalling, and reminiscent of that felt by the most ardent Nazis against the Jews. It goes beyond reason and Western logic, but it is real, and will have to be dealt with not only for the duration of the Gulf War, but for generations to come. Americans may feel that the hatred is unjustified or misdirected—it does not matter. It exists, and it will affect the outcome of the Gulf War.

Culture clash

Winning wars is a matter of choice and of will. The clash of arms in the Gulf is also a clash of cultures, and victory or defeat will depend upon the strength of will of each of those cultures, and how each culture will choose to express its will. One culture—Saddam Hussein's—has indicated exactly what its course of action will be: to set up a primitive blood bath in the sand, and let the forces of the coalition drown themselves in it. Spokesmen for the United Nations coalition have repeatedly indicated that every effort will be made to minimize the loss of life on both sides—

To many Arabs, the United States is a hated enemy. These pro-Iraqi protesters gathered in Amman, Jordan, on January 14, 1991.

an unprecedented approach to war, and one that must give the Iraqis comfort.

Television screens have been filled with images of high-technology weapons operated by highly dedicated, marvelously skilled Westerners. The other side of the coin—the low-tech Iraqi warfare of infantrymen hunkered down in fortified trenches, of tanks buried hull down in the sand, of millions of mines sown in great huge cordons across the desert—is not telegenic, but it may be even more important to the war's outcome.

Only the iron core of the Iraqi Army, the Republican Guard, is composed of professional troops whose business is fighting. Most of the rest are impressed recruits. These troops have been ordered to "hunker down," to fight from fortifed positions. The fact that they are unwashed and poorly fed doesn't matter to them, because they

War in the Gulf   27

In Desert Storm, as in all wars, much of the burden falls to ground troops. These 82nd Airborne paratroopers were snapped in Saudi Arabia.

are terribly aware of how limited their options are. If they stay and fight and live, they will be heroes. If they die, they will go to Paradise as martyrs. But if they flee, if they desert, they will be killed—and lose Paradise forever.

Their task is relatively simple: to die while making UN forces die at a rate that will sap the Western will to fight, to convert the Kuwaiti desert into a modern-day Verdun.

The Verdun allusion is apt, for the situtation in which the Iraqi troops find themselves is not unlike the situation that faced troops on the Western Front during World War I. What was it that kept men in the trenches under savage fire for days on end, enduring the worst privations, seeing their friends killed? Fear and fear alone. The Tommy, the *landser,* the *poilu,* each man, no matter what his nationality, knew that while death was probable in the trenches it was *certain* for desertion. The hapless Iraqi soldier knows the same.

And yet events so conspired that this is the only way that the Gulf War could be fought. In the nearly 50 years since the end of the Second World War, the UN coalition forces have perfected weapons that cause the greatest destruction to the enemy while incurring the fewest casualties to themselves. Trillions of dollars have been spent on smart bombs, stealth aircraft, body armor, main battle tanks, and an unimaginable array of similarly modern devices. Iraq, while it has spent billions on armament (it is the largest purchaser of arms in the world), cannot hope to match the West gun for gun, jet for jet, missile for missile.

Instead, it intends to shift the war's focus from technology to blood, to which it is inured. In the business of shedding blood, Iraq has a tremendous advantage in experience—killing is a part of Iraqi life, whether in the war with Iran, on the streets of Kuwait, or in the dungeons of the *Mukhabarat,* the Ba'th party intelligence unit that polices the army, the civil service, and the general populace.

The deadly game

In many ways the Iraqi-UN confrontation is a game of chance in which the betting chip is the killing level. The first bets have already been placed: high technology against passive targets. It is an elegant way to conduct war, and there is very little killing. But the tactic has not been immediately decisive, so the next level of betting may be exactly what Saddam Hussein wants: hand-to-hand fighting against defended positions.

If the UN succeeds in this difficult role, Saddam Hussein will then raise the ante to chemical and biological warfare. If the UN fails, and withdraws, Saddam will have won.

If the UN fails in close-quarters combat and chooses *not* to withdraw, then the next level of bet must be made, and the West may be moved to play its trump card: the nuclear attack. It may be that the bunkers from which Saddam directs his war could survive such an attack, but his troops and his people do not have bunkers and they could not survive.

The penultimate question is: What does the kill level have to be before (a) the UN coalition breaks up or (b) it resorts to the ultimate weapon?

The ultimate question is: If the coalition has made a decision to see the war through, and to stay at all costs, why not employ nuclear weapons first, and avoid the various levels of killing—particularly of Americans—in between?

Fortunately there is another, more optimistic solution—a scenario in which the West carries on its air attacks until it achieves absolute aerial supremacy, and then sets up a vast gunnery range in the Kuwaiti desert, to pry the Iraqi tanks and troops out of their bunkers one by one. This approach takes longer and isn't as certain as other methods, but it might avoid international outcry. And it is certainly better than to be sucked into an endless meat grinder of a ground war.

The airpower option

The process for this is simple, economic, and, in the end, merciful. Having established air

The North African struggle between British forces and those of Germany's Erwin Rommel (center) during World War II is the West's most recent experience with desert warfare.

supremacy, a continuous combat air patrol is flown to protect against sudden attacks. Then the full weight of modern technology is brought to bear, as reconnaissance planes and satellites map the desert area as carefully as observation planes were used during World War I to plot the trenches.

The full weight of airpower is then levied against each Iraqi site, first with carpet bombing by B-52s, followed by precision strikes by fighters vectored in using the most recent information on new targets.

When this process exhausts all evidence of enemy activity, huge propane bombs could be dropped, wiping out any residual resistance. Then and only then would it be correct for the coalition to send in ground troops.

The hazard here of course is that for every day of the Gulf War that goes by, the risk of massive Muslim-nation defections from the coalition increases. There could also be deliberate, savage treachery from Syria. But these are probably more acceptable risks than the consequences of an Allied nuclear attack.

The high tech/low tech scenario has been played before, on a far less grand scale. Most recently, it was carried out for an excruciating eight years between Iraqi and Iranian forces. Generally, though, high-tech elements came into play only occasionally during the Iraq-Iran war; most of the fighting was deadly low tech—the machine gun, the mortar, the artillery shell.

The most recent example in Western experience was during the Second World War in North Africa. Allied control of both the air and the sea meant that Rommel's Afrika Korps was faced with an ever increasing Allied numerical and technical superiority. When the Afrika Korps had the fuel to be mobile, it was able to survive at a relatively low casualty level. When the fuel stocks ran out, it simply dug in and died.

The communications miracle

One of the first objectives of the Allies' high-tech war in the Gulf has been to take out the Iraqi command and control centers. Considerable effort was expended, and considerable success obtained, but the fact is that eight years of experience with similar attacks had conditioned the Iraqis, who knew that redundancy of communications systems was the key, and that in a pinch an intact telephone line could be as valuable as satellite communications.

As sophisticated as military communications are, the high degree of technology and efficiency

ALLAH'S HELP IS ALL SUFFICIENT FOR US

In a remarkable illustration of the power of modern communications, Saddam Hussein prepared an address for broadcast to the American people following Iraq's invasion of Kuwait.

of everyday commercial media has been astonishing. For the first time in history, an enemy news team—in this case reporters from CNN—was allowed to broadcast directly from a city under attack. Even more remarkable, that same agency was granted an interview, to be broadcast to the American public, by an enemy leader, Saddam Hussein.

Television has given the world other images of the Gulf War. Less spectacular than some, perhaps, but more moving, are the on-the-spot scenes of fighter pilots taxiing in after a mission, adrenalin bulging their veins, smiles lighting up their faces. (The communications miracle does not end there, either, for any of these pilots could have left his plane, walked to a telephone, and spoken with his family, almost immediately.)

For the first time, too, television has given America and the world a clear view of the well-trained women of the U.S. military services going

American women have come to the fore as soldiers in the Gulf War. This Air Force lieutenant colonel, assigned to duty in Saudi Arabia, was separated from her 5-year-old daughter.

crisply about their business, from flying transports to loading bombs to servicing radars. Even Saudi Arabian culture shock caused by this sort of female activity has been captured on video.

One of the greatest services of the media during the Gulf War has been to place America's leaders, including President Bush, Secretary of Defense Richard Cheney, General Colin Powell, General H. Norman Schwarzkopf, and others on the line for interviews. The grilling can be rough, and the interviewees are all pros, able to waffle a point if they have to, but never has a public been so well served in terms of information.

Equipment and morale

Yet in the end, it is neither television nor high-tech equipment that will solve the Gulf conflict. In the end, it boils down to a matter of the troops, the men and women of the coalition forces versus the soldiers of Iraq.

The first and greatest difference between the two forces, one that is not stated often enough, is that the U.S. troops that form the majority of the coalition force are all volunteers, a factor of inestimable value in terms of morale. These men and women *want* to be doing the job they have been called upon to do.

Morale also depends upon confidence in training and in equipment. For the most part, American troops accepted that their training was the best available given the fact that munitions had become so expensive that practice firing might be limited to only one round a year. But the entire universe of American armament was suspect after years of adverse commentary from the media and Congress. Almost every weapon system in the U.S. arsenal had been held up for ridicule. Confidence was bound to be eroded.

Yet from the very first day of Operation Desert Storm, it was evident that America's considerable investment in equipment and training had paid off. Perhaps the most crucial evidence, and certainly the most visually exciting, was the way in which U.S. Patriot missiles countered the Iraqi-launched Scuds. The thoroughly satisfying

As if the heat of the desert were not bad enough, Allied soldiers must be prepared for chemical warfare. Uncomfortable anti-gas suits and masks can save lives, but they hamper movement and limit a soldier's capacity to fight.

images of the Patriots reaching up through the mist to merge with the Scuds were matched in intensity by the pride on the faces of the troops operating the equipment, a pride that seemed to say, "By golly, it did work after all."

More than just fighting equipment has become remarkably sophisticated. In many ways, perhaps, the greatest difference in Western and Middle-East culture may be seen in the lavish consideration for personal comfort given the UN forces, particularly those of the United States. Even the seemingly mundane elements of the coalition soldiers' daily lives have reached a level undreamt of by the Iraqis, or by soldiers past. For example, combat sanitary facilities during World War II ran somewhat to slit trenches and G.I. helmets, the latter the universal container for head, hot water, and food. Today these have been replaced with air-transportable showers, tables with wash basins and mirrors, and industrial style "Porta-Potties."

But these are "home base" luxuries that will not be able to go forward in the sand at the moment the coalition ground forces mount an attack. Instead the troops will strip down to the bare necessities, which are far different today than they were a desert war ago. Now the troops have to be prepared for chemical warfare, and be able to don grotesque anti-gas suits on a second's notice.

The challenge of desert combat

In heat that may reach 120 degrees and higher, the Allied soldier will have to place *over* his existing equipment a helmet cover, an overgarment,

A plentiful supply of water is vital to the well-being of soldiers fighting a desert war.

rubber outer boots, gloves, and a gas mask. The 15-pound anti-gas suits were originally designed to be worn for as long as ten hours—in a European climate. In the desert, the heat may sap body fluids at a rate that would make more than an hour inside the suit impossible, for under a real attack, it would be impossible to break the seal of the garment to replenish those fluids.

Active fighting in the desert requires that each soldier take in as many as five gallons of water a day, weighing 40 pounds, far more than he could carry on his person. That means that resupply has to be close to the front lines, vulnerable to the same chemical attack that the soldier is.

Just as sand and heat can grind a human down, so can it insidiously destroy electronics, engines, and even such seemingly invulnerable items like the barrels of cannons. The best optical sights in the world can be fooled by the shimmering heat radiating from the desert surfaces.

Evil ambition

Saddam Hussein has made an assessment that he can become so barbarous, that he can sacrifice so many lives, that he will be able to secure Kuwait as his country's "nineteenth province," and a lion's share of the world's oil supply. More amazingly, he feels that he can do so to the abject approval of most of the Muslim population of the world. Having done these things, he can turn his malignant energies to the intimidation and coercion of the entire Middle East. If the UN coalition and the U.S. forces have withdrawn, who will stop him? And once in control in the Middle East, what price might Saddam then exact from a world still hungry for oil?

The Gulf War will not have a tidy ending like the conclusions that relieved the world on November 11, 1918, and on May 8, 1945. The world has changed since those days and become infinitely more complex. The neat ending may be a thing of the past. Whatever the outcome of Operation Desert Storm, the Middle-East struggle will go on, in a multiplicity of forms, into the next century, and perhaps beyond. The world's best hope is that America and its allies remain at the ready.

NATION PROFILES: WHO'S WHO IN THE GULF WAR

United States

The history of United States interest in the Middle East may be said to have begun in war against perceived piracy. In 1805 President Thomas Jefferson, hearkening to the new American tradition of "millions for defense but not one damn penny for tribute," sent an American fleet to rescue hostages held by the Barbary Coast pirates based in North Africa—and incidentally destroy the sailing vessels the Arabs used.

Prior to the Second World War, American involvement in the region centered around oil interests, typified by a joint agreement signed by Standard Oil of California and Saudi Arabia in May 1933. This agreement, like others in the area, was advantageous primarily to the producing company and the rulers of the oil-producing nation. Typically, such agreements provided the company with full discretion over production and pricing, and was valid for an average of 80 years. In the case of Saudi Arabia, major oil find "Dammam No. 7" in 1938 assured its future as an oil-producing country—and assured the West's continued interest.

One of those interests was in maintaining low oil prices, and the price per barrel remained remarkably constant over the years, never venturing much above the $2.50 mark until growing discontent, international inflation, and the increasing power of the members of the Organization of Arab Petroleum Exporting Countries (OPEC) in 1968 forced the price "all the way" to $3.73 per barrel by 1973. There have been considerably greater upward fluctuations since.

The second United States experience in combat in the Middle East was during World War II, and by coincidence, the initial effort was once again on the North African coast. But it was in the postwar years when the U.S. slowly began to assume the mantle of leadership that was slipping from the tired shoulders of the British Empire. It was then that U.S. involvement in Middle Eastern affairs became complete and—because of short-sighted alternative-fuel policies—irrevocable.

Containment of communism

Curiously enough, the American engagement with Middle Eastern powers did not originate with American thirst for oil, but instead as a result of the United States' policy of containment of communism. As Great Britain's power faded, and as the Soviet threat to "the Northern tier" of Greece, Turkey, and Iran loomed larger, the Truman Doctrine was formulated in 1947. Essentially, the United States offered these nations economic and military assistance in return for help in containing Communist expansion. The Doctrine was well received and worked because the recipients of the aid perceived the same threat, and felt a natural alliance with the United States against an old enemy. In short, the Doctrine's tenets met regional interests, including

Egyptian president Jamal Abdel-Nasser was a politician very much in the American mold: forceful, charismatic, and able to inspire his people. His relationship with the Soviet Union disturbed the West.

those of Iran, where a friendly regime was ensured by restoring the Shah to power.

Yet Russia was able to hurdle the Northern tier. Its move into the area was well handled and ably orchestrated by the emerging leader of the Arab world, Jamal Abdel-Nasser, the President of Egypt, who had confounded the West by concluding an arms agreement on a massive scale with the Soviet Union in 1955.

Nasser soared like a rocket on the Arab horizon, reaching his highest point with the nationalization of the Suez Canal in July 1956. France and England, stung by Nasser's decidedly uncolonial action and troubled by the prospect of possible Soviet domination of the area, conspired with Israel to forcibly retake the canal, resulting in the Suez conflict. England's Prime Minister Anthony Eden, after years of standing in Winston Churchill's shadow, had his great chance at history, only to fail miserably in the face of both Soviet and U.S. opposition. Britain's attack on Egypt was aborted; so great was Eden's fiasco that Nasser maintained his luster as a great Arab leader, despite the savage drubbing Israel had administered to his forces.

In January of 1957, President Dwight D. Eisenhower formulated the Eisenhower Doctrine, using essentially the same philosophy as the Truman Doctrine, but for a far different audience. By this time, it was considerably more difficult to find compatible national interests in the Middle East. First of all, the widespread sympathy of the United States public for the valiant little "underdog," Israel, was evident. Second, U.S. interest in the area was too strongly reminiscent of Great Britain's heavy-handed colonial policies over the years, and Arab patriots were not anxious to be seen merely exchanging one set of economic handcuffs for another.

Also, to the revolutionary elements within the Arab nationalist movement, Communist doctrine was not as unattractive as it was to Greece, Turkey, and Iran, all of whom had had bitter experience with it. Turkey was especially resistant to communism, not only because of past conflicts with Russia, but because of a desire since the 1923-38 rule of Turkish president Kemal Ataturk to become more Western.

In its essence, the Eisenhower Doctrine called for Middle Eastern states to be content with an informal pattern of Western control, and to accept American economic and military aid in exchange for Arab willingness to become a part of the Western bloc that restrained the Soviet Union. Unfortunately, the Eisenhower Doctrine was as fatally flawed as the Truman Doctrine had been on the mark. There was no evidence whatever that the Arabs perceived the Soviet Union as a threat anywhere near as great as that of Israel, of Iran, or even of some of the inter-Arab alliances.

Instead, the Arabs correctly saw that the two great powers, the United States and the Soviet Union, could be played against each other, while furthering Arab aims. Perhaps the greatest manifestation of this was Eisenhower's insistence on Israel's withdrawal from the Sinai, reluctantly carried out in the spring of 1957, to the undoubted satisfaction of the Arab states.

Israel goes to war

The effect of the Eisenhower policies was to cause Israel to immediately begin to look abroad for sophisticated arms to match the Soviet weapons provided to Egypt. France became Israel's intimate trading partner, with Ouragan and, later, Mystere jets, and a wide variety of high-technology equipment.

This escalation continued until 1967. In the interval, the Palestine Liberation Organization (PLO) had been created, the radical wing of the Ba'th Party had taken over in Syria, and in an attempt to stem his decline in prestige, Nasser had prevented Israeli ships from entering the Gulf of 'Aqaba. The Israeli response was the preemptive strike that became known as the Six Day War, in which Israel successively defeated Egypt, Syria, and Jordan. Israel occupied the whole of the Sinai Desert to the Suez Canal, the Golan Heights, and the West Bank of Jordan.

After 1967, U.S. aid to Israel increased on a vast scale, to offset the frantic resupply of arms that the Soviet Union was furnishing the Arab states. Perhaps the only encouraging thing in the entire period was the fact that the Soviets were making exactly the same mistake that the United States had, assuming that the supply of

Egyptian soldiers taken prisoner during the 1973 Yom Kippur war sit under Israeli guard.

arms and technical advice would purchase loyalty from states whose goals and needs were vastly different from the donor's.

Yet for the next five years, as Egypt and Israel waged a war of attrition, Egypt became Russia's client state, just as Israel became the United States'. At the same time, the U.S. was engaged in building up Iran's strength, obviously intending for the Shah to become America's primary advocate in the area by making Iran a Middle East superpower.

There was yet another Israeli-Egyptian conflict, this one the Yom Kippur War of 1973, carefully planned by Nasser's successor, Anwar Sadat, and coming within hours, perhaps, of being successful. The Israelis were resourceful enough to once again pull their chestnuts out of the fire with brilliant fighting and superb tactics, but they were badly shaken. And once again there began a massive resupply of armaments by the U.S. to Israel, this time even as the fighting was going on. The resentment felt by the Arab world toward the U.S. was tremendous.

The first oil crunch

Many Arabs believed that the ultimate success of the Israelis in surviving and then winning the Yom Kippur war was the U.S. airlift of first-line equipment that began on October 12, 1973, followed by a $2.2 billion aid package a week later. The Arabs responded with an economic bombshell loosed upon the entire world, but one that shook the United States badly then, and continues to shake it to this day. Six OPEC members met in Kuwait and raised the price of oil from $3.01 to $5.12 a barrel. By December, the price had shot up to $11.65, and it was evident to everyone that Middle Eastern politics and economics had entered a new era. The fallacy of the Eisenhower Doctrine was never more evident, for the Shah of Iran had been the leading advocate for higher oil prices.

In response, the United States began some tentative alternative-fuel programs, and made serious and lasting efforts to reduce energy expenditure.

Arms for sale

The concept of containment of the Soviet Union was now vastly complicated; not only did the "evil empire" have to be contained, its massive armament program had to be matched, as did its export of arms to countries all over the world. The two great powers had at last stumbled upon policies that met the felt needs of the countries of the Middle East—massive arms sales of increasingly advanced and increasingly expensive weapons. The Middle East became the world's principal market for arms and military equipment, and the Soviet Union became the

History in the making: Anwar Sadat, Jimmy Carter, and Menachem Begin at Camp David.

world's biggest arms exporter, followed by the United States.

The Middle Eastern countries, newly enriched by the black gold that commanded ever higher prices, spent a great portion of their income on arms, but still had funds left over for foreign investments and improvement of their homelands. The bonanza was not without its problems, however: The higher prices led to over-production and a leveling and then a drop in oil prices. In time, the drop was sufficient to make the United States, in a most short-sighted fashion, abandon most of its alternative-fuel plans.

Amidst all of this turmoil, there emerged one of the signal events of statesmanship of the century—the journey of Egyptian leader Anwar Sadat to Jerusalem in November 1977. His trip initiated a search for peace that overlooked the Israeli excursion into Lebanon in 1978, and that was brought to a conclusion in September of that year in the United States, where President Jimmy Carter mediated the Camp David accords.

During the same period of time, the United States supplied arms for the first time to Egypt and Saudi Arabia. This marked the beginning of a political, economic, and military wooing that reached its peak with the events of the 1991 Gulf War.

Bad news from Iran

Despite massive efforts by the United States to shore up the Shah in Iran—efforts made in spite of the Shah's greedy position on oil prices—the Pahlavi dynasty was overthrown in January of 1979, beginning a new era in U.S.-Iranian relations.

The country that was to have become a surrogate U.S. superpower and the bulwark of American efforts to contain Soviet encroachment in the Middle East was now openly America's bitter enemy. The bad state of affairs was dramatically illustrated in November 1979, when the U.S. Embassy in Iran's capital, Tehran, was attacked and its personnel seized as hostages.

America reacted to the events in Tehran with hatred and aversion. Islamic fundamentalism was alien to American culture, and the events taking place in Iran seemed inexplicable. Many Americans felt that the Ayatollah Khomeini, Iran's spiritual leader, must be a madman intent on dominating the entire Middle East.

President Carter, deeply aware that his triumph at Camp David had been irrevocably damaged by the hostage situation in Tehran, proclaimed in 1980 a "Carter Doctrine," announcing that the United States would resist, by military means if necessary, any attempt by any power to "gain control of the Gulf Region." Carter was triply concerned. First, his Presidency and reputation were being held hostage by the Ayatollah as surely as the American citizens in Tehran were being held. Second, Russia had taken advantage of America's distress to launch its invasion of Afghanistan (an action similar to the Soviet Union's treatment of the Baltic states as the Gulf War erupted in 1991). Third, Iraq, seeing Iran to be in disarray, launched an invasion of Iran. As a footnote, one might add that the respective invasions by Russia and Iraq were later proved to be as insanely counterproductive as the American involvement in Vietnam had been. Regardless, these actions signaled deepening trouble in the Middle East.

Botched rescue

Despite the enunciation of his Doctrine, President Carter did not have the means to implement it, short of using strategic nuclear weapons. His unilateral disarmament policies had compromised U.S. strength. There was no such thing as a "Rapid Deployment Force," and American military strength everywhere was depleted. Perhaps the whole American defense situation was best summarized by the abortive April 1980 attempt to rescue the hostages—an ill-planned and ill-executed fiasco that ended with American helicopters burning in the desert.

More than just helicopters burned, however, for the Middle East was suddenly transformed from a region of essentially inter-dynastic focus—a place where tribe competed against tribe—to a place of vast ideological confrontation between fundamentalist revolutionary Iran and the other, essentially conservative Gulf regimes.

The United States was suddenly beset by a wide spectrum of Middle Eastern problems that encompassed the increasingly truculent rumblings of Colonel Qaddafi in Libya, the persistent Arab-Israeli confrontation, the demands of the Palestine Liberation Organization, the concerns about Iran and the Iraqi invasion, and Soviet activity in Afghanistan.

A minor chord to the major themes of this agonizing symphony was struck by increasing oil prices. The squabbling Arab nations could not agree upon production levels, and thus could not completely control world oil prices, but prices rose to $28 a barrel in May 1980, and to $32 in December. The OPEC nations were beginning to conduct colonialism in reverse—and it hurt!

New Gulf alliances

A collateral product of the tensions of the time, one which would have tremendous import for the United States in 1991, was the formation in 1981 of the Gulf Cooperation Council (GCC), made up of representatives of Saudi Arabia, Kuwait, Bahrain, Qatar, and the United Arab Emirates. It was in this organization of wealthy but peaceful states that the first steps were taken toward mutual defense, steps that would ultimately form the foundation for the coalition of states at war with Iraq. (Ironically, the GCC members received substantial aid and military training from Jordan, one of the few Arab states to stand openly with Iraq in the 1991 Gulf War.)

Another organization important to the current conflict grew out of the understanding displayed by President Hosni Mubarak of Egypt, who succeeded Anwar Sadat. Mubarak has sought to

Disaster: Workers carry a body from the rubble of the 1983 terrorist bombing of the U.S. Marine barracks in Beirut.

preserve the peace with Israel, friendship with the United States, and continued rapprochement with the Arab world. In doing so, he established a moderate bloc that reached all the way from Saudi Arabia and Jordan on one hand to the PLO and Iraq on the other, primarily to form a counterweight to Syria. Such is the power of Mubarak's quiet personality that recent turbulent events have seen a complete revision of the status quo, with Syria now part of the anti-Iraq coalition. Mubarak remained at all times a staunch friend of the United States, even as the eight-year Iraq-Iran war gave his country an even greater position of leadership in the Arab world.

America stirs, the Soviets sputter

The span of the Iraq-Iran war coincided almost exactly with the unprecedented build-up of American military might at all levels during the Reagan administration. In that eight-year period—a short time when looked at in the context of modern weapons of war—the U.S. gained enormous strategic and tactical strength, along with the ability to deploy forces on short notice. At $2.4 trillion, the build-up was costly indeed, but the positive results speak for themselves.

Those achievements are more impressive if they are examined against an economic background. In the period under discussion, the Soviet Union spent *500 billion more dollars* on defense expenditures than did the United States. In doing so it spent itself into an economic grave, in a process that shook the Iron Curtain off its hooks, ended the Cold War, liberated many of the Eastern European countries of the Warsaw Pact, and profoundly affected the Soviet system.

In all, it is clear that the basic functioning of the U.S. Department of Defense and of American industry during the period of military build-up was far better than critics imagined. This is not to say that there was no waste, no fraud, no bureaucratic stupidities. It *is* to say that on balance, the funds were well spent, well managed, and well proved by the results.

Bush's resolve

The same years of the Reagan administration and the Iraq-Iran war saw a reversal of the "malaise" of the American people that had been perceived by Jimmy Carter's speechwriters, as well as a complete reversal in attitude toward individuals in the U.S. military. And in the very strange way that history has of anointing the unlikely, it fell to President George Bush to put those forces to use when at last a situation irredeemable by diplomacy arose.

George Bush—himself a combat veteran—has risen to the challenge of Iraq's invasion of Kuwait, providing cool, well-reasoned leadership.

Bush, a veteran combat pilot, successful businessman, consummate politician, and (to the surprise and consternation of political cartoonists) an effective leader, has quietly placed his personal stamp on the successive maneuvers that established an unprecedented coalition in the Gulf. This coalition encompassed not only the members of the GCC, but also radical Syria, conservative Turkey, reluctant France, and sensitive Saudi Arabia. In the process Bush has secured pledges of economic aid from those rich near-superpowers, Germany and Japan. At the same time, he has exerted his will on a Congress that was initially anxious to distance itself from the prospect not only of war, but of the taxes a war brings.

President Bush did not deviate an iota from his original principles—that Iraq must leave Kuwait and restore the legitimate Kuwaiti government—principles for which he received United Nations endorsement. He said that if Saddam Hussein did not comply, he would take military action, and the world for the most part did not believe him. Yet military action came "sooner rather than later," as Bush had stated.

In the entire progress toward the war, the President did not foreclose on peace; he encouraged every mediator, no matter how remote the prospect of success. But when the time came, he exercised the prerogatives authorized by the Congress and by the United Nations, and attacked Iraq exactly as he had forecast—with full force, with full regard to civilians, and with extreme precision.

Perhaps more incredibly than anything else, the Bush administration actually seems to have learned something from the Vietnamese war. It is obvious that the President has carefully avoided many of the errors of that era—pointless and misleading emphasis on body count; over-euphoric reporting; and the worst, most deadly and deplorable error of all, Defense Secretary Robert McNamara's famous and, in the end, fatal philosophy of "graduated response."

Instead Bush has chosen an array of specialists who have adhered loyally to the official policy, but who have had wide discretionary powers of a nature unheard of at the time of Vietnam.

Bush's team

While standing before the press at frequent intervals, President Bush has left the majority of the war reporting to Secretary of Defense Richard Cheney, and the Chairman of the Joint Chiefs of Staff, General Colin Powell. These two men have worked smoothly in directing the war effort, and effortlessly in smoothing the war news.

The cooperation is reciprocal; Powell had demanded that if the United States were to intervene, that it should do so on a rapid and

Defense Secretary Richard Cheney (left) and General Colin Powell are key players in the Desert Storm campaign.

massive scale. He also insisted that if war came that there be no hesitation to use all the forces available to win it.

Powell, the son of Jamaican immigrants, grew up in New York, and began his meteoric rise as a White House fellow in 1972. The first black—and the youngest man—ever to become Chairman of the Joint Chiefs of Staff, Colin Powell may well become the United States' first black Vice President, if not the first black President.

Following President Bush's lead, Cheney and Powell have delegated both responsibility and authority to the officers in the field. As Commander in Chief of American military forces of the Desert Storm force, General H. Norman Schwarzkopf must not only direct the military operations of the troops but act as the senior diplomat on the spot to deal with the sensitive issues posed by working with the coalition.

Command of all U.S. forces in the Middle East is held by General H. Norman Schwarzkopf, who must walk the tightrope of military and diplomatic necessity. From the start, he refused to be lured into a premature ground war.

Known variously as "Stormin' Norman" for his pedal-to-the-metal methods, and as "the Bear" for his six foot three inch, 240-pound physique, Schwarzkopf has tailored his own personal style to meet the needs of the situation. With an army of eager young American men and women suddenly placed in the Islamic culture of Saudi Arabia, Schwarzkopf will require all of his ability as a soldier and a diplomat to keep things harmonious.

But perhaps more heartening than the President's deft deferral to Cheney and Powell and their own regard for Schwarzkopf has been the portrayal of the American fighting man and fighting woman on the instant replay of the war that graces the television screens every evening. We see faces buoyant with triumphant victories scored in the air and we see tense faces awaiting an incoming Scud. These are the real players, the front-line people, and they symbolize better than any politician, any flag-rank officer, or even any network anchor just how deep is the American commitment.

What's at stake

Inevitably, the sight of such men and women raises the question of values. Is it worth risking their lives and spending so much money (perhaps $600 million per day) to fight such a war? What has the United States to gain? What has it to lose?

The losses are easiest to count. The United States could lose prestige, power, influence, and money. If it moves out of Saudi Arabia, Iraq will move in and control nearly 45 percent of the world's oil. Saddam Hussein will become an oil czar—not a pretty prospect.

The United States would also lose credibility with its allies. But more important, it would lose credibility with its enemies. Moving out of Saudi Arabia would be far different than moving out of Vietnam. Leaving Vietnam meant economic gain; leaving Saudi Arabia would be an economic catastrophe.

But beyond that, the United States would lose moral stature. If Kuwait is absorbed and Saudi Arabia conquered, could the members of the Gulf Cooperation Council, Syria, Jordan, Israel, indeed, even Egypt and Iran, be far behind? This is not a domino theory, it is an osmosis theory. The greed of Saddam Hussein would strain through borders like moisture through a membrane.

And what has the United States to gain? The reverse of all of the above, of course; increased

America agonized over its prisoners of war. This is Navy pilot Lt. Jeffrey N. Zaun.

credibility, increased power, influence, and even, at some distant point, an improved economic situation.

But far more importantly, the United States would end the 20th century as it began it, as a symbol of hope for the downtrodden, as a country brimming with idealism. A just peace in the Gulf will do more than create a true golden age in the 21st century for the United States; it will be the basis for a new order throughout the world.

Iraq

Iraq has many similarities to Germany, not least of which is the indefensible geographic location it occupies, the keystone linking Iran, Turkey, Syria, Jordan, Kuwait, and Saudi Arabia.

In ancient times it was known as Mesopotamia, "the land between the rivers," nestled between the Tigris and the Euphrates and a natural invasion route for any passing conqueror. Over the centuries, the country has been occupied by no less than seven invading forces—Persian, Greek, Roman, Arab, Mongol, Ottoman, and British. Each invasion left its effect upon the current population.

Unlike many of its Middle Eastern neighbors, however, Iraq has been blessed by nature with fertile land, ample water in the central area, and many natural resources, including, of course, vast petroleum reserves that currently approach 100 billion barrels. Its population of about 19 million could have expected to enjoy a true golden age in the 21st century, if almost continuous war, oppressive regulation, and absolute political indoctrination had not been its lot.

Total control

But circumstances have never been ordinary for Iraq, conditioned by its past to expect hardships, and now steeped in the strange political philosophy of Saddam Hussein's rigorously controlled organization, the Arab Ba'th Socialist Party. The Ba'th party offers an ephemeral mixture of nostalgia for an Arab world of strength and unity that never existed, as well as exhortative demands for self-sacrifice for the future. In many ways, Ba'thism echoes the "Ein Volk, Ein Reich, Ein Fuehrer" slogan of Nazi Germany, calling as it does for an Arab nation stretching from Iraq to the Atlantic Ocean, crying out against the defilement of this "homeland" by imperialism and Zionism, and putting Saddam

Saddam Hussein, seen here at an Arab summit before the war, dominates Iraq completely; internal opposition to his rule is crushed mercilessly.

Hussein's presence everywhere. You see the face of Hussein at every turn—in the media, on posters, in architecture and sculpture (his brawny forearms—some say even the whorls of his fingerprints—are reproduced in the memorial celebrating Iraq's 1988 "victory" over Iran), and even in the sky, in uncanny laser light shows.

The Ba'th party—once closely allied with the ruling Ba'th party in Syria—has quite literally consumed the state and is today a well-functioning police vehicle for Saddam Hussein, a means to choreograph both public opinion and public demonstrations. Hollywood choreographer Busby Berkeley might have had dozens of dancing girls, but he was never able to put together the legions of arm-shaking, fist-waving, shouting Ba'thists that Hussein can conjure up for television.

Invasion and turmoil

Crisscrossed by invaders, Iraq became part of the great Muslim empire in the 7th century.

From the 8th to the 13th century, there blossomed in Baghdad the "Golden Age of Islam" that produced tremendous and lasting effects upon the arts and sciences. In 1258, however, another invader came, this time the Mongols led by Hulagu, the grandson of Genghis Khan. Baghdad was completely destroyed.

There followed almost 300 years of tribal turmoil until, in 1534, Baghdad fell to the Ottoman Empire, where it remained, with brief exceptions, until the end of World War I. During the nearly 400 years of Ottoman rule, tribal strife was encouraged as long as the modest taxes were collected.

But by the end of the 19th century, Iraq's position along the route to India gave the British concern. Having alienated the Turks, Great Britain was worried that Germany might extend its influence into Iraq and Iran, threatening India, the jewel in the crown of the British Empire. Great Britain decided to act pre-emptively, and invaded and occupied much of Iraq as soon as World War I broke out in 1914.

By 1916, Britain and France had agreed that Iraq would remain in the British sphere of influence, an agreement confirmed at the San Remo conference in 1920. England approached the task of control with an eye on efficiency and economy. Instead of attempting to administer the country as it did India, it installed the Hashimite Prince Faysal as King. British advisers made virtually every important policy decision.

Independence and oil

Iraq became an independent nation in 1932, but still hewed strictly to the British line. Oil had been discovered in Iraq in 1923, and even a British Empire caught in the throes of the world's economic depression was not going to relax its hold on potential wealth. Not unnaturally, anti-British feeling was strong throughout Iraq, particularly in the army, and there began a series of coups of the sort that has characterized Iraqi politics to this day.

In 1941 a pro-German coup ousted the British loyalist Prime Minister General Nuri al-Said; England responded immediately with an invasion that restored Nuri to his position. From then until 1958, Iraq was marked by a reasonable degree of political stability.

In July 1958 the "Free Officers" group of the Iraqi army led a revolution that swept away not only the King and Prime Minister but also any vestige of British influence. The leader of the new republic was Brigadier 'Abd al-Karim al-Qasim.

Saddam's rise

Saddam Hussein was 21 years old at the time. Orphaned at the age of nine months, he was brought up by an uncle who taught him the guerrilla techniques against the British. Poorly educated, Saddam Hussein was rejected when he asked to be admitted to the Baghdad Military Academy; the situation was reminiscent of Adolf Hitler's rejection by Vienna's art schools, for Hussein always aspired to be a soldier as Hitler aspired to be an artist. Yet Saddam's only contact with armed combat was assassination, the first instance being his attempt on Qasim's life.

Wounded, Saddam escaped and eventually went to Egypt, where he admired the charismat-

Iraqi militiamen on the march, chanting, "We would rather die than be on our knees."

ic Pan-Arab leader, Jamal Abdel-Nasser. He returned to Baghdad in 1963 after a Ba'ath coup had ousted Qasim. Hussein began to lay the careful foundation for his present position by establishing a militia for the Ba'th party, which had taken power permanently in 1968 after a flirtation with the local Communist Party.

Hussein began a stealthy rise to power, maintaining a low profile while simultaneously strengthening his grip on the party as he strengthened the party's grip on the country. In 1979 he was secure enough to assume the role of President and Commander in Chief. He became president at a time when the rise in oil prices had brought wealth to the country beyond any previous conception—oil revenues had increased tenfold from 1972 to 1974, and had gone up steadily since then.

So if Saddam Hussein's informal control had been strong before, it now became absolute as he ruthlessly suppressed all opposition. It became death for anyone, famous or humble, to say a single word against the new "Father-Leader."

Twelve days after his inauguration as President, for instance, he ordered the execution of 22 highly placed government officials, including members of the Revolutionary Command Council Cabinet and some of his closest personal friends. Reportedly, many were killed by his own hand. His purge extended to the army, trade unions, student movements, and government officials at the lowest level; at the same time he demonstrated largess by raising salaries of the military, civil service, police and intelligence services, and allocated $80 million to religious sites and the care of pilgrims. He even launched a cultural campaign to restore Babylon and its legendary gardens.

Whether such cultural improvement is sincere or mere ploy, in the end it is made irrelevant by Saddam's savagery. Mass murder is the act of a madman—or of a man brought up in a culture alien to the West, accustomed to acting pragmatically, absolved from any moral imperative but his own self-interest. Hussein has been described as a cold-blooded thug to whom human life means nothing, qualities amply illustrated in the bloody war against Iran that he launched in 1980.

Iraq and Iran at war

The Ayatollah Khomeini, flushed with his long-awaited ascension to power in Iran in 1979, had railed against the Sunni rulers of Iraq, and called for a Pan-Arab return to Islamic fundamentalism. But the Ayatollah's own campaign had completely disrupted Iran's structure; in overthrowing the Shah he had reduced Iran's military capacity to a negligible level, and

Basra, Iraq, like much of Iraq and Iran, suffered terribly during the Iraq-Iran war.

Hussein thought the country was ripe for the picking.

The rivalry between the two nations was of long standing, extending back to the 16th century. Over the years the reasons for the disputes have remained unchanged—boundary disputes, access to the sea, concern about colonial alignments, and access to religious sites. One permanent source of trouble was the control of the Shatt al Arab estuary, which governed access to the Gulf itself. The increased power of the Shah—power derived from the United States— had enabled Iran to support the Kurdish uprisings within Iraq, weakening the still-forming regime. Ultimately, Iraq was forced to accept Iran's demands on their boundaries and for access to the Shatt al Arab.

Iraq had initially announced its only intentions to be the acquisition of the other half of the

Shatt al Arab and some disputed border territory. But bolstered by the success of his initial surprise attack, Hussein began to portray the captured Iranian areas in neighboring Khuzistan/Arabistan as a province of Iraq, a tactic that was to loom again in 1990. In addition, he spoke of the appropriation of Iranian oil, and tried to divide the Iranian people from their religious rulers.

But the Iranians rallied as the Iraqi military appeared to be uncoordinated and irresolute. Slowly the tide turned against Iraq, so that in 1984 Hussein was to say victory for Iraq meant merely "defending ourselves until the other side gives up."

In eight years of war, Iraq poured out more than $112 billion in expenditures, while being denied billions more in revenues from its shutdown oil fields. One hundred twenty thousand young Iraqi soldiers died in battle. During the long eight years, both countries endured an endless exchange of artillery fire at the front and missiles in the cities, Iraq firing 200 into Iran, and Iran firing 70 in return. Iraq employed poison gas against Iranian troops—and against its own people, the Kurds, who had seized upon the war to rebel.

The Iraq-Iran war extended to other countries as well. By 1987, Iraq was able to strike 76 ships in the Straits of Hormuz, while Iran struck 87; mines and missiles became threatening to the other Gulf states. Russia and the United States became increasingly involved in retaliatory acts, including one gross error when an Iran Air airliner was shot down by an American missile. The airliner was confused with an Iranian F-14 fighter plane supposedly inbound to attack. In another eerie forecast of the future, on May 17, 1987, an Iraqi Mirage warplane fired two Exocet missiles into the USS *Stark*—an "accident" for which Hussein apologized.

Exhaustion finally caused the war to grind down; a cease-fire took effect on August 20, 1988.

Grip of terror

One war had ended, leaving Iraq exhausted and billions of dollars in debt. Saddam Hussein now portrayed the war as a heroic struggle in which Iraq had stood alone against the tide of Arab fundamentalism—which meant that Iraq's war debts should be forgiven, and a sort of Arab Marshall plan be instituted to pay for its losses and rebuild the country. When the response to his plea was inadequate, Saddam Hussein turned to the invasion of Kuwait as the easiest way to replenish his fortunes.

How is it that the intelligent, vigorous people of Iraq will endure, and (on camera, at least) support a man who has suppressed their freedoms, sacrificed their youth, destroyed their economy, and alienated them from the world?

The answer is terrorism, pure and abject, yet a terror that permits the most heartfelt of the national needs, adherence to the Muslim religion, and that offers in an incidental way as many creature comforts as can be allowed after the nation's military programs are accommodated.

The exercise of unremitting terror is made easier by the traditional divisions that exist within the nation. About 75 percent of Iraq's population is Arab, 18 percent are Kurds, with the remaining seven percent divided among Persians, Armenians, Turcomans, and other ethnic groups.

Iraqi Foreign Minister Tarik Aziz meets the press. Like every member of the Iraqi government, Aziz is a puppet of Saddam Hussein, and functions mainly to express Saddam's will.

Ninety-seven percent of the population is Moslem, with about 65 percent being Shi'a and the remainder Sunni. It is more than a religious division however—it is also a class division, with most of the Shi'a earning their way as farmers, unskilled laborers, shepherds, and, increasingly, as soldiers. The Sunni dominate all of the professional classes, and the Ba'th party.

The most troubling faction to Saddam Hussein, of course, are the proud Kurds, who are also found (and are also troublesome to the local government) in Syria, Turkey, and Iran. The Kurds—most of them Sunni Moslems—have a separate language and culture, and fight for self-determination, taking aid from Iran or the Soviet Union as they can get it. In repressing the Kurds, Saddam has used every weapon at his disposal, including poison gas that killed 4,000 civilians in a single attack at Halabja, Iran.

Baghdad, once the cultural center of all Islam, has become an echo chamber for Saddam Hussein's speeches, a house of mirrors for his images. He has established complete personal control over the lives of those around him, a control that extends like the divisions of a pyramid

The world was horrified in January 1991, when Iraq released an enormous spill of oil into the waters of the Gulf. Wildlife like this helpless cormorant suffered terribly.

tree into the smallest aspect of Iraqi life. There is no deputy, no second in command except in the titular sense. Everyone is a puppet to Saddam's will.

The press and many public figures have compared Saddam Hussein to Hitler and the Ba'th party to the Nazi party. In the diplomatic interval before the Persian war began, there were many allusions to the democracies' 1938 negotiations with Hitler at Munich. Hitler's brutalization of the terrain of Europe seems to have found its modern counterpart in Saddam's callous engineering of a calamitous oil spill into the Gulf in January 1991. Yet the hope of the people of Iraq, and of the world, should now center around another echo from the German past, the brave resolve of Count Claus von Stauffenburg, the man who came closest to assassinating Hitler. Perhaps the answer to the current tragedy lies not so much in UN resolutions, or in the armed might of the United States and its allies, but in the moral courage of an individual who will not permit Saddam Hussein to continue his murderous path to power.

Win-lose scenarios

Iraq obviously considers that it has everything to gain if it merely survives the Gulf War, and does not admit defeat. But an out-and-out Iraqi victory would allow Saddam Hussein to become the preeminent Arab leader, one who unquestionably would wish to add Saudi Arabia to his territory, and who would then solve the Palestinian question by eliminating Israel.

An Iraqi loss would force Iraq out of Kuwait, and make it forfeit its position as leader of the Arab conservatives. Iraq would become prey to a revived Iran, which almost certainly would rush to fill any power vacuum. It now seems obvious that if Iraq is defeated, it will lose Saddam Hussein—a happenstance that may be perceived by the people of Iraq as true victory in defeat.

Kuwait

The innocent cause of the current war in the Persian Gulf may fairly be laid to a tiny country smaller than New Jersey, but possessed of wealth beyond the dreams of avarice. Kuwait lies at the head of the Gulf, close to the Shatt al Arab estuary that was the heart of the Iraq-Iran disagreement that helped trigger the eight-year war that erupted in 1980.

Kuwait's background can be traced to a federation of tribes that founded the kingdom in 1716, Kuwait then being an obscure fishing village. In the subsequent years, several waves of emigrating tribes took successive control of the area, which, as the port facilities were developed, became primarily a mercantile community. The land was mostly unsuitable for agriculture, so fishing and pearl-fishing were the principal industries until the entire Kuwaiti world was turned upside down with the discovery of the Burgan oil field—then the largest in the world—in 1938.

Unlike most of the colonial countries, Kuwait was led by men who had actively sought to be placed under British protection, which was reluctantly granted in 1914. But when oil prospecting began, British interest increased, and the Kuwait Oil Company was formed with typical concessionaire rights and privileges.

Independence and wealth

The Suez conflict of 1956 inflamed the Kuwaiti desire for independence, which was granted by Britain in 1961. Iraq immediately laid claim to the area, and it was necessary for Britain to deploy its forces to defend against the threat.

Kuwait's oil industry was nationalized in 1975 and the Kuwait Investment Office began to funnel the incredible proceeds into foreign investments, estimated to total more than $100 billion in holdings in the United States, Europe, and Asia. (That staggering round number is coincidentally also the amount that some attribute to the *personal* holdings of the ruling al-Sabah family.)

The amount of foreign investment, immense as it is, assumes an even more fundamental importance when it is realized that the investments earn approximately 85 percent as much revenue as was being earned by the oil fields before the Iraqi invasion. This was truly a case of riches squared.

Members of the Kuwaiti Army Martyrs Brigade participate in post-invasion maneuvers in Saudi Arabia.

Kuwait has a population of a little over two million, and the oil had brought the lives of Kuwaiti citizens to a degree of state-supported wealth beyond the dreams of any Utopia. There were no taxes, and education and medical care were free.

Kuwait's population is more mixed than those of other Arab countries; only 28 percent of the people are Kuwaitis; 39 percent belong to other Arab nationalities, 9 percent are South Asian, 4 percent are Iranian, and fully 20 percent are from other countries. Kuwait is 85 percent Muslim, of which 30 percent are Shi'a and 45 percent Sunni.

So wealthy was the country, and so widespread was the government's largess, that only 20 percent of the labor force was Kuwaiti—all the rest was foreign labor, which did not share equally in the welfare benefits accorded citizens.

Young Kuwaiti protesters express their opinion outside the Kuwaiti Embassy in London.

One of the problems that had vexed the Kuwaiti government, and was not solvable by the mere application of money, was the influx of Palestinians, as well as the location within the country of members of terrorist groups. Both conditions posed problems that were solved temporarily by Saddam Hussein's invasion.

Under invasion

To the great credit of the Kuwaiti military, the August 2, 1990 invasion by Iraq was spotted immediately, and the Emir, Sheik Jabir al-Ahmad al-Sabah and his family, were able to flee to Saudi Arabia by helicopter. Kuwaiti forces put up a brave fight (the Kuwaiti Air Force flew two strike missions against the invaders in the first —and only—morning of combat) but to no avail. The Emir's younger brother Fahd was killed at the Palace.

Exiled Kuwaiti leader Sheik Jabir al-Ahmad al-Sabah met with President Bush in Washington following Iraq's invasion of his country.

Now Kuwait waits, its country savagely assaulted. In the first hours of the invasion, every conceivable luxury, from Mercedes automobiles to kiwi fruit, was stolen and sent back to Iraq. The ruthlessness reached heights improbable even for Saddam Hussein, when it was reported that 300 newborn infants had been taken from their incubators and left to die. The incubators were shipped back to Iraq.

What peace may bring

In Hussein's eyes, Kuwait no longer exists; it is the 19th province of Iraq. The question remains for the world to ponder—how badly destroyed will Kuwait be when Iraq is forced out—will there be a country left for the Emir to return to?

If Kuwait's sovereignty is restored, and the ruling government reinstated, Kuwait's oil revenues will in time be sufficient to restore the country as it was before the invasion. However, Iraq's departure may well herald the arrival of Iran, and the entire process could begin again. And if Iraq remains, all of Kuwait will become raw material for the Iraqi war machine, and the former idyllic life of the Kuwaiti citizens will be little more than a dimly remembered dream.

Great Britain

England dominated every aspect of the Middle East for centuries, as the British Empire spread its red colors across the maps of the world. England explored the Middle East, claimed its territories, exploited its resources, and used it as a strategic base to balance the influence of the Turkish Ottoman empire and to pursue a pair of 20th century wars against Germany.

Somehow, England never came to rule the Middle East as it had ruled India, with pomp and circumstance so powerful that when India did become independent in 1948, it continued to follow much of English practice in language, education, law, the military, and business. India was the jewel of the Empire. The countries of the Middle East, in contrast, were regarded by Britain as merely useful, productive, or strategic—but never with the same close regard that was felt for India.

Protecting the Empire

Yet Egypt, along with the Suez Canal and, later, the countries of the Gulf with their invaluable oil resources, would become critical to the Empire. The result was that, in two world wars, Great Britain poured out its wealth and blood in the desert sands of the Middle East and North Africa. It was defending its own interests, of course, and even may have felt that it was also protecting the native populations from even more exploitative countries of the day—Turkey and Germany during the first war, Germany and Italy in the second; the populations' view on this protection was never solicited.

In 1914, Great Britain was to foreshadow the events of recent years when it delegated to the Government of India the task of seizing Basra and the Shatt al Arab waterway, with a view to protecting the local oil supplies.

The initial success of British arms led to excessive optimism, and a decision was made to march on Baghdad, and thus deal a mortal blow to Turkish prestige. The march across harsh desert landscapes became an agony—temperatures reached 120 degrees and the troops, poorly equipped for the expedition, suffered dreadfully. When winter came, the torrents of rain caused the marshlands to flood, and the troops who dropped out, plagued by cholera and dysentery, were murdered by Arab scavengers who followed them. England found itself hopelessly embroiled in a war from which it could not disengage.

This hideous start to Britain's Middle Eastern military adventure at the outset of the First World War foreshadowed not only the four hard years of fighting that followed, but also the bitterly protracted events of World War II. It does not, one can only hope, foreshadow the events of the Gulf War.

T.E. Lawrence

A more influential World War I campaign was conducted by the British in Palestine, a campaign that was to have incalculable effect upon the future. It was there that Captain T. E.

Captain T.E. Lawrence—better known as Lawrence of Arabia—led Arab forces to brilliant triumphs over the Turks during World War I.

Lawrence led the Arab tribes of Sherif Abdullah and Amir Faysal in revolt against their Turkish overlords. Lawrence used his desert forces as a British admiral might have used ships, ignoring the ground features, flowing around strong points, striking at strategic targets. The tactics were perfect for his time and his troops; they unfortunately became the standard for the British Army for the early part of the Second World War, where they proved to be more than inadequate—they were in fact deadly wrong.

By 1918, more than 98 months of fighting had been conducted (compared to only 35 in the same theater during World War II). The Turks had been driven from the area, and former British prime minister Arthur Balfour had already made the commitment that a Jewish homeland was to be provided in Palestine.

World War II in North Africa

In the Second World War, the Middle East and North Africa were the primary ground battlefield for England until the Allied invasion of Normandy on June 6, 1944. The war in North Africa was important for a number of reasons. Given the inability of the British to open a second front in Europe, it was essential to offer at least indirect support to the Russians by conducting land operations against the Germans. Hitler always regarded the African theater as secondary, and refused to give to his commanding general, Erwin Rommel, sufficient troops to win the campaign.

To England, and the Commonwealth troops, the theater was a godsend, for it pitted them primarily against the ill-equipped and poorly motivated Italians, who sometimes had to queue up to surrender.

The North African campaign was a godsend for British morale as well, for after three years of suffering one defeat after another at the hands of the Germans, the 1942 battle of El Alamein marked the turning point of the war. In the larger sense, England had not won a battle before El Alamein; afterwards it did not lose one.

As noted previously, England began to disengage from the Middle East after the end of the Second World War, as its empire began to fragment, and as nationalist movements took hold everywhere. In 1956, Britain made an abortive attempt to reassert its influence in the Suez Crisis, was admonished by the United States, and withdrew.

Britain's stake

So it is especially noteworthy that in 1990, at the outset of the United States' time of trial with Iraq, England was staunchly at America's side. Led by Prime Minister Margaret Thatcher, England unequivocally sided with the United States position from the first day of the crisis, and brought its superbly trained troops—the "Desert

British prime minister John Major greets the Desert Rats—the British 4th Armored Brigade—in Saudi Arabia.

Rats"—into the theater immediately, along with the brutally effective Royal Air Force. And although there was a change of British government when John Major succeeded Mrs. Thatcher as Prime Minister, England remained steadfast.

Iraq's ejection from Kuwait will add to the luster of English military history, and almost certainly provide a spur to English industry. If Iraq remains in Kuwait, its power unimpeded, England and the rest of the world will be forced to turn to alternative fuels to avoid a slow slide into economic slavery administered by Iraq.

Saudi Arabia

Saudi Arabia has never been a colony of another nation, which partially accounts for the proud nature of its people, but more pointedly indicates why it is better able to get along with Western powers.

Nevertheless, it is difficult for a Westerner to conceive of the size, desolation, and isolation of a country so immensely wealthy as Saudi Arabia. A little less than one quarter of the size of the United States, it has a harsh, dry desert climate. There are no rivers and rainfall is almost non-existent except in the very tip of the Saudi Southwest. The country of over 17 million people is 100 percent Muslim. Ninety percent of the people are Arab and ten percent Afro-Asian. The Arabs are the proud descendants of tribes that have roamed the peninsula since ancient times. The name Saudi Arabia is derived from the name of its first ruler, King Abd al-Aziz bin Abd al-Rahman Al Saud—later known as Ibn Saud—and the history of the country is essentially the history of the Saud dynasty.

Ibn Saud was one of the handful of truly great Arab leaders of this century, looking every inch the regal Arab king. A huge man, good humored, he had many wives and as many as 80 children, in keeping with good Muslim tradition. Unlike most Arab leaders he recognized the need for foreign assistance, and foreswore the customary Arab chauvinism to seek out friends in the West.

Big money, big spending

All Saudi Arabian life changed when oil was discovered in 1933, and a concession agreement with Standard Oil of California was signed. By the early 1940s, explorers had found the enormous Abqayq field, larger than any ever found in the United States. This discovery came at a time when farsighted American businessmen realized that the U.S. was about to shift from an oil-exporting to an oil-importing status.

Saudi Arabia's King Fahd has successfully linked his nation's destiny to that of the West.

The sudden wealth of the new nation was wasted almost as profligately as the oil that brought it. Over the years, from 1932 on, almost one-third of the tremendous Saudi revenues were devoted to the purchase of military equipment. On a per capita basis this was the highest ratio in the world, twice as high as Israel's, and three times as high as the United States'. Yet over the years graft and waste have resulted in the Saudis fielding of only relatively modest combat forces.

So great was the waste that the Kingdom edged toward bankruptcy during the early years of the 1960s; national currency, the riyal, had to be devalued, and an appeal made to the International Monetary Fund.

The Saudis rebuild

In 1964, Prince Faysal, who had demonstrated remarkable skill in revitalizing the economy, succeeded his father King Sa'ud. King Faysal changed Saudi Arabia overnight from a debtor nation on the brink of revolution to one of the most stable regimes in the Middle East. He did it in part by setting an example of austerity and moral rectitude.

Later in his reign, as Saudi Arabia began to realize some of the benefits of the oil boom, King Faysal began a conscientious development of a modern infrastructure of business, education, medical services, and, above all, education.

At the same time, he felt that the two greatest threats to his state and to Islam were communism and Zionism. He resented particularly Israel's denial of access of the Aqsa Mosque to millions of Muslims, and was incensed by the displacement of Palestinians.

King Faysal was assassinated in 1975 by a mentally unbalanced relative, and was succeeded by an equally pious, very sensible man, King Khalid. The entire government remained very much a family affair; Khalid's brother, Crown Prince Fahd, became first deputy Prime Minister. In 1982, King Khalid died of a heart attack and was succeeded by Fahd.

King Fahd was well trained to bring Saudi Arabia along in a turbulent world. He saw that his country's place derived solely from its oil exports, but he went beyond most Arab leaders in his thinking by realizing that the customers for his oil—the United States and the rest of the free world, primarily—were also his best defense against communism. In addition, with foreign investment soaring to a point beyond $60 billion, Saudi Arabia obviously had a deep interest in the health of the Western economy.

A Saudi fighter pilot gives a wave after clambering into his American-made F-15 Eagle.

Fahd's dilemma

This reality led to one of King Fahd's most significant concerns—the perception of his country's actions in Muslim eyes. In Saudi Arabia are found the two holy cities, Mecca and Medina, which annually draw people from all over the world on the Hajj, the Muslim pilgrimage that is one of the pillars of their faith.

Thus when Saddam Hussein not only invaded Kuwait, but rolled his armed forces to the Saudi border, he imposed an almost impossible task upon King Fahd—not only to ask for active Western intervention, but to allow Western military people—men *and* women—to operate from the sacred Arabian soil, without defiling the great religious sites and customs.

Conservative and deeply secular, Saudi culture suffered an unbelievable shock when it met the American presence in Saudi Arabia. Jews had been forbidden from the nation's borders, yet American Jewish soldiers were coming to protect

The Saudi capital of Riyadh has been a target of Iraq's erratic but dangerous Scud missiles.

it. Women were supposed to wear clothes that covered them completely, yet American women soldiers—wearing fatigues and carrying the eternal symbol of Arab manhood, the rifle—were flooding in.

As a tribute to both countries, there have been very few incidents. Part of the reason for this is an incredible profession of humility on the Saudis' part—not a customary Saudi characteristic. Saudi commentators openly admitted that the Saudi defense posture was a sham, that Saddam could destroy them in an instant, and that they needed the U.S. protection.

The simple, and now admitted truth, is that nothing in the Saudis' training or background would allow them to contest the Iraqi army on anything like an equal basis. One problem is the tribal nature of the Saudi military—royal bloodlines count for more than ability.

Saudi Arabia's future

The disinclination of the Saudis to defend themselves with the same degree of ferocity that the Iraqis almost certainly intended to bring to an attack against them has engendered some adverse comment in the United States, where the question is asked whether Americans should die as substitutes for Saudi soldiers. It is an unanswerable question—American soldiers are there not to die for the Saudis but to protect American interests.

For if the Americans had not intervened, in company with the UN coalition, Saudi Arabia would have been gobbled up by Iraq in a twinkling, and the Sahd family exterminated.

The question must arise as to Saudi Arabia's course of action when Iraq is ejected from Kuwait. Then the full measure of the country will unfold, for it must on the one hand seek to prevent Iran or any other nation from filling the military vacuum that will be left by the Iraqi withdrawal, while on the other it will have to dig deep into its resources to pay for not only the expense of the war, but also to repair the ravages in Kuwait.

France

France's experience in the Middle East began with Napoleon's abortive and costly invasion of Egypt in 1798. The French occupied parts of the country for three years, and exposed Egypt to Western ideas and technology. In 1830, France invaded Algeria, and began a vicious campaign to kill the indigenous population, a campaign similar to the exterminating Indian Wars in

North America. The natives were slaughtered, the land expropriated and given to European occupiers for settlement. France offered French settlers free land, free transportation, seed and livestock, and then saw to it that their products were brought in duty free. More than 150,000 immigrants had come to this old "new world" by 1850, and more than 550,000 by 1900.

Harsh rule

The French were haughtier, more exploitative, and more cruel masters even than the British. Algerians were forced off their property and made subject to severe discrimination. Discouraged from attending the schools established by the French, the Algerians found their traditional Moslem schools closed. So complete was the French control that Algeria came to be regarded as an integral part of Metropolitan France, with the native Algerians looked upon as inferior beings subject to rigorous controls. In the process, three million of the natives died, their tribes were destroyed, and their very way of life eradicated as the production of wine superseded the production of cereals and other agricultural consumables.

Algeria merely whetted France's appetite, and in 1881 a pretext was found for annexing Tunis, which became a French Protectorate. Yet the French influence in Tunis was never carried to the extreme that it was in Algeria, and an internal resistance movement soon developed, a movement that would seek complete independence. Led by Habib Bourguiba, the great Tunisian statesman, the movement achieved this goal in 1956.

French president Francois Mitterrand worked hard to avoid war, but brought France into the coalition when diplomacy failed.

Such a movement took longer to foster in shattered Algeria, and it was not until about 1950 that the full fury of the now urbanized Algerian population began to be felt. A savage civil war from 1954 to 1962 shattered both Metropolitan Algeria and France; independence was finally awarded in July of 1962.

French Syria

France undertook yet another abortive colonial relationship in 1920. In the customary manner in which the winners of the First World War defied their own often professed insistence on self-determination, France was awarded a Mandate over Syria. Opposition was intense and hostile, and France approached the problem by playing on the multiple divisions in Syrian society, a technique the Syrians would learn and apply down through the years to the long agony in Lebanon.

A long series of minor revolutions, each one led by different tribal or religious leaders, led ultimately to a major rebellion in 1925, when Druze tribesmen were able to displace the French from numerous towns and villages in the Syrian countryside, and even attempt to take over Damascus. French military power drove them out, but it was evident that independence must someday come.

The fall of France to Nazi Germany in 1940 inspired Syrian nationalists, who were able to bully the vacillating, totalitarian Vichy French government into concessions. Under Charles de Gaulle, the Free French offered independence as a means of securing Syrian support. Independence was granted in name in 1941, but was not in fact fully achieved until 1946, when the French withdrew from the country.

France is not noted for its cooperativeness—as an example, when the United States made its air strike against Libya in 1986, the French would not allow overflight of its territory.

Glory and reality

Yet the diplomatic efforts of President Bush and Secretary of State James Baker seem to have made the correct impression upon France's President, Francois Mitterrand. Despite (or, in retrospect, because of) Mitterrand's efforts to make peace until the last moment by personal negotiations with Saddam Hussein, he perceived that "not one gesture, not one word from the President of Iraq has given us a glimpse of a hope of reconciliation." With that, he committed French Armed Forces to the coalition.

France, like every industrialized nation, has much to gain if the Middle Eastern status quo is restored, and Iraq is not utterly destroyed. Because of its vast nuclear power network for

French sailors assemble aboard the aircraft carrier Clemenceau *as it heads for the Gulf.*

energy, France is not quite as dependent upon oil as some of its allies. But it is desperately dependent upon those allies as customers, and could not stand to see them forced into bankruptcy by an Iraqi victory.

And there is something else that must surely motivate the French. The baton that Napoleon said every French soldier carried in his knapsack is still there; when the tri-color is unfurled above Middle-Eastern sands, France thrills to another time and to another beat—that of *la gloire*—glory.

Italy

If France's excursions into colonialism in the Middle East and North Africa were disastrous, those of Italy turned out worse, even though Italian colonial management was more adroit, and less cruel, than France's.

In Italy, the same sort of colonial lobbies that had inspired France's actions in Algeria and Tunisia were pressing for their own African land to exploit. As the grip of the Ottoman Empire began to loosen in the Middle East, the Italians decided that they could risk an invasion of Libya in 1911, incidentally employing aircraft for the first time in combat.

The invaders were successful only in occupying the coastal towns for many years; the tribal forces resisted any incursion to the Libyan interior until the early 1930s.

Mussolini's dreams of glory

By then the Italian dictator Benito Mussolini was intent upon creating a new Roman Empire, and from a foothold in Italian Somaliland he launched his invasion of Ethiopia in 1936. The Italian Army, to uninformed eyes well equipped and well led, eventually subdued the largely defenseless Ethiopians. *Il Duce* had defied the League of Nations, thumbed his nose at France and England, and created, as he proclaimed from his famous balcony, a new Italian Empire.

The empire lasted only until early 1941. The British, thirsting for a victory after more than a year of war, attacked westward from Egypt into Cyrenacia. Led by the 7th Armored Division "Desert Rats," the English destroyed nine Italian divisions and took 130,000 prisoners. A simultaneous attack was launched against the Duke of Aosta's 100,000 troops in Ethiopia and Italian Somaliland. By April 4th, 1941, Addis Ababa had fallen and the British had captured 50,000 additional prisoners. The Italian Empire had ceased to exist.

*Giulio Andreotti,
prime minister of Italy,
heads a vital
industrial power that
is an important part of
the Allied coalition.*

A newer, better Italy

But Italian commercial interests persisted, and the need for the Middle East as a market and as a source of fuel became critical to Italy. Eager to redeem national prestige when the Gulf confrontation arose, Italy presented a solid front with the United Nations coalition.

But even more important was a realization that the Italy of today is a far different country than the Italy of Mussolini. It is now a ranking industrial economy, rather than an agrarian one, with a per capita output equivalent to France or England. At about $19 billion, its annual defense expenditures constitute almost three percent of its gross domestic product.

Much of that defense expenditure goes for its membership in NATO, and its participation in the development of new weapon systems with other countries. And it is perhaps a commentary on this Italian dedication to a responsible military renaissance that an Italian was among the first pilots to fall in the war.

Israel

Israel is a tiny land. If one excludes the occupied territories, it is about 250 miles long, and ten miles wide at its narrowest point. The question of the occupied territories is a difficult one. Jimmy Carter's 1978 Camp David accords, which were reaffirmed by President Reagan's 1982 peace initiative, indicate that the final status of the West Bank and the Gaza strip will be negotiated among the concerned parties. Whether this will be relevant or not in the future depends very much on the outcome of the 1990-91 Gulf War.

Lying at the eastern end of the Mediterranean, with borders adjacent to Lebanon, Syria, Jordan, and Egypt, Israel was plucked from Palestine in 1948 at the end of an improbably successful war of independence. It is a country founded and sustained by immigrants; some 500,000 Jews had arrived by 1948; in the years that followed, another two million arrived.

With them they brought the apprehensions of years of their own trials and tribulations. Even more significantly, their arrival was met with massive Arab discontent, for the homeland they occupied had also been the homeland of the Palestinian people. Another, perhaps even more sensitive point is that the Jewish faith now intruded on Muslim holy places. The importance of this resentment is amplified by the fact that 17 percent of Israel's population is Arab, mostly of the Sunni Muslim faith.

"Born in battle"

Israel proudly claims to have been "born in battle" and in the intervening four decades has

Israeli prime minister Yitzhak Shamir epitomizes the toughness and fortitude of the Israeli people.

fought four more wars to preserve its independence. In addition, it has had running wars of attrition, undeclared but terribly bloody, both along its Egyptian border and in Lebanon.

Just as Egypt's Nasser is a father figure to that country, so is David Ben-Gurion a hero to Israel. This kindly, grandfatherly man became Prime Minister and Minister of Defense in 1948, and molded Israeli society to his vision.

Certain that the Arabs would never genuinely accept Israel, Ben-Gurion decided that an intimidating armed strength was the only key to Israel's survival. It was Ben-Gurion who laid the foundation for Israel's military superiority, but it was also he who saw to it that similar excellence was achieved in science, industry, and education.

Israel returned to the battlefield successfully in 1956 and 1967, each time defeating Arab coalitions unable to match the efficiency and élan of Israeli forces. Each war increased Arab resentment, and made the possibility of peaceful

U.S. Patriot anti-missile launchers, deployed in farmland near Tel Aviv, Israel.

settlement even more remote. Unable to disarm despite its victories, Israel saw more and more of its disposable income going into high-tech weapons. Each time the Arabs lost, they turned to the Soviet Union for reequipment with ever more sophisticated weaponry. It was a vicious circle that has not ended, and that may never end.

The enmity felt by Arabs toward Israel became useful to the leaders of Arab countries. To be accused of being "soft" on Israel was tantamount to treason. When there were national troubles, an attack on Israel, verbal or military, was an easy way to divert attention.

The circle of antagonism was broached somewhat when, as alluded to earlier, Egyptian president Anwar Sadat made the peace overtures that led ultimately to the Camp David accords. But some Middle Eastern leaders, including Saddam Hussein and the Ayatollah Khomeini, never deviated from their intense, almost hysterical hatred of Israel. Perhaps the most cynical expression of this was an assurance by Tarik Aziz, Iraq's For-

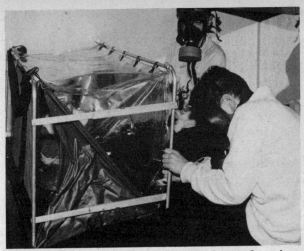

Mindful of possible chemical attack, two boys in Jerusalem close toddlers into a protective tent.

eign Minister, who blithely told the world following his nation's invasion of Kuwait that Iraq would launch an unprovoked attack upon Israel if Iraq were confronted in the Gulf.

The endless fight

Aziz was as good as Saddam Hussein's word, and the Scud missiles began pouring down on an Israel that demonstrated an unbelievable degree of restraint. Despite this restraint, and despite Israel's obvious fortitude and toughness, the question arises as to what Israel would lose if Iraq were to win the war, and become the dominant Arab nation. The answer is clear: Everything. And if Iraq loses the war, Israel will probably gain little except the opportunity to continue fighting for its existence.

Jordan

Jordan is a land of great antiquity, ringing with biblical names like Gilead, Amman, Moab, and Edom. Slightly smaller than Indiana, bordered by Syria, Iraq, Saudi Arabia, and Israel, its three million people are as sharply divided as the history that shaped the nation.

Jordan came under Muslim influence in 636 A.D. Subsequently it was ruled by a variety of tribal chieftains until becoming part of the Latin Kingdom established in Jerusalem by the Crusaders in 1099. Saladin, the sultan of Egypt and Syria from 1174 to 1193, was the next conqueror; he was followed by a 400-year reign by the Ottoman Empire.

Like many of the other countries in the area, Jordan's modern identity grew out of the break-up of the Ottoman Empire in 1918. Arabs led by Amir Faysal, and advised by Lawrence of Arabia, conquered much of the area of Jordan, only to have their country divided by the infamous Sikes-Picot agreement of 1916. This secret arrangement divided the regions of the area known as Levant between the French and the English. France obtained control of what is now Lebanon and Syria, while all the territory from Palestine to Iraq fell within the British sphere of influence.

At that moment, no one except perhaps the Amir Faysal considered Jordan to be a separate entity. Arabs considered it to be a part of greater Syria; the British—particularly the European Zionists—considered it part of Palestine.

In an effort to suppress the rising tide of Arab nationalism, Great Britain offered independence

King Hussein of Jordan has attempted to balance the desires of his pro-Iraqi people with his wish to avoid alienating the West.

to what became known as Transjordan in 1923, with Amir Abdallah as Chief of State. There followed almost 20 years of British tutelage and influence, as Amir Abdallah began to define not only his country, but his ambitions for empire by taking the Hijaz from Saudi Arabia, and reestablishing his brother as King in Syria.

When World War II erupted on the scene, Transjordan was in a position to play an important local role. The British-trained-and-led Transjordanian Arab Legion was the region's most effective Arab fighting force, and it was used in 1941 to suppress a pro-Nazi revolt in Iraq.

In 1946, Transjordan achieved full independence, and Abdallah became king. Immediately upon Israel's declaration of independence in 1948, the Transjordanian Arab Legion joined Egypt, Syria, Lebanon, and Iraq in war against the new Jewish state.

It was not until 1950 that King Abdallah annexed the West Bank and changed the name of his kingdom to Jordan. It was a case of the mouse swallowing the cat, for there were now more Palestinians in his new country than there were Jordanians.

King Hussein walks the tightrope

The present King Hussein assumed control as a teenager in 1953, and fought again against Israel in 1967, losing the West Bank and impairing forever Israel-Jordanian relations. From the debacle there also came the creation of the radical, militant Palestine Liberation Organization, intent on securing an independent Palestine even after two wars had failed to bring this about. One of the results, costly to King Hussein's prestige in the Arab world, was his suppression of a vicious civil war instigated by the PLO in 1970.

Jordan did not participate in the 1973 war against Israel, and began to further its already good relations with the United States. It seemed, until August 1990, that King Hussein had succeeded in walking the terrible tightrope between hatred of Israel, Jordanian desire to recover the West Bank, fear of the Palestine Liberation Army, and fear of Iraq. His popularity at home and abroad had never been greater.

Yet when the Gulf War came, he was placed in an impossible position, caught in the crossfire between Iraq and Israel. His own people admire Saddam Hussein, for his defiance both of the United States and Israel, and King Hussein has listened to them. The concept of linkage between the Gulf conflict and the Palestinian question is undeniably appealing to him. The question that arises is how long can his balancing act go on?

Assuming King Hussein can maintain his balance, the after-war consequences for his nation do not look bad. If Iraq wins in the Gulf, Saddam Hussein will undoubtedly reward Jordan for its loyalty. If Iraq loses, King Hussein's long track record of stability and good sense will quickly win back for Jordan any friends he has lost.

Egypt

Egypt has been inhabited for more than 8,000 years, and was the site of one of the greatest civilizations of all time. Islam arrived in Egypt during the 7th century, and today 94 percent of Egypt's almost 55 million people are Muslims.

In terms of geography, Egypt is made up almost solely of desert and the life-giving Nile Valley, where good water and fertile land have been enough to sustain the nation down through the centuries.

Like other Middle Eastern lands, Egypt has seen a variety of conquerors, passing successively through Greek, Roman, Byzantine, Arab, Ottoman, and British occupiers.

The quest for Egyptian independence began at the time of the Versailles conference in 1919, but England, which had invaded the country in 1882, had no intention of relinquishing control of the Suez Canal, that vital link to India and Southeast Asia.

Appearances were served in 1922 and 1936 by treaties granting limited technical independence to Egypt, but the British remained firmly in control. Farouk, young son of King Fu'ad, succeeded his father as King of Egypt and the Sudan in 1936, and proved to be as weak and dissolute as the British could have wished.

The British gave up all thought of surrendering control when World War II began, even though the native Egyptian population was solidly anti-British and would have welcomed a

German victory and the deposition of King Farouk.

The ascendance of Nasser

A genuine revolution occurred in 1952, engineered by an organization known as the Free Officers. Nominally led by General Muhammad Naguib (one of the few officers in the 1948 Arab war against Israel who had acquitted himself well), the Free Officers in 1954 chose the charismatic Jamal Abdel-Nasser to head the new regime.

Nasser was brilliant, charming, hardworking, and appealing not only to the Egyptian *fellahin*—the peasant class upon which everything depended—but to the Arab world, of which he became the undisputed leader.

Nasser's resources did not match his aspirations, however, and he lost wars to Israel in 1956 and again in 1967, somehow retaining his position of leadership. When he died in 1970 he was succeeded by Anwar Sadat, a very different sort of man, but in many ways a greater statesman. His Yom Kippur attack on Israel came close to succeeding, but when it did not he turned to diplomacy and reversed the tide of violence in the Middle East by agreeing to President Carter's mediation in the Camp David accords.

Sadat was assassinated in 1981, and was succeeded by Egypt's present president, Hosni Mubarak. A low-key personality compared to his predecessors, Mubarak has not been able to maintain either Nasser's or Sadat's position in the Arab world because of his continued friendship with the United States, and his peaceful relations with Israel.

Thanks to the brilliance and inherent appeal of Egyptian president Jamal Abdel-Nasser, Egypt became the leader of the Arab world in the 1950s.

Mubarak's gamble

It is all the more noteworthy that Mubarak, in the face of Iraq's invasion of Kuwait, elected to join the UN coalition and send forces to Saudi Arabia. In doing so he has placed his position on the line; if Iraq wins, he will be forced out of power. If Iraq loses, Mubarak will still have to find a way to explain to other elements of the Arab world that in a crisis, he opted to fight with the United States against an Arab nation. It will not be easy.

Germany

Germany finds itself overtaken by internal events impossible to have imagined even two years ago—the reunification of what had been a forcibly divided nation is now an accomplished fact, and Germany must now deal with the problems of assimilating the tired, wheezing, Trabant-like East German economy into its own flourishing system.

At the same time, the most delicate possible international situation has arisen for the Germans. The Gulf War pits Germany's true and great post-war friend, the United States, against Iraq, in defense not only of Kuwait and Saudi Arabia, but also of Israel. Germany joined the UN coalition with some hesitance, but has declined to send any troops, citing constitutional prohibitions against doing so.

Bad memories

At the same time, Germany has received wide publicity for having supplied Iraq with the chemical elements necessary for conducting chemical warfare, an issue about which everyone is sensitive, but particularly the Israelis. Germany is also supposed to have provided the technical assistance necessary for the construction of the elaborate bunkers that provide Iraqi dictator Saddam Hussein with near-perfect security against even nuclear attack. Bunkers and poison gas are clearly not buzz words with which Germany wishes to be publicly associated.

In partial response, Germany has given to the coalition more than two billion dollars in equipment—most of it obsolete East German materiel—and has promised an additional five and one half billion dollars in cash. In early February of 1991 Germany promised to send to the Gulf 30 tons of oil booms and skimmers to combat the enormous oil spill that had been engineered by Saddam Hussein the previous month. Additionally, Germany has agreed to send 600 troops and their flak equipment to its World War I ally, Turkey. Germany has also offered to provide Patriot missile batteries to

German chancellor Helmut Kohl heads the most prosperous nation in Europe. But for all of Germany's economic success and political clout, the nation finds that old memories are difficult to erase.

Israel, together with the troops to man them; Israel accepted the missiles and declined the troops.

The question now remains as to how the world will view Germany as the Gulf War progresses. Is Germany still digesting its reunification and too preoccupied to participate more actively? Is it hesitant to show any overt militaristic tendencies? Perhaps it is merely content in the knowledge that, no matter what the outcome of the Gulf War, the German economic miracle will likely go on.

Libya

Libya is the fourth-largest nation in Africa, slightly larger than Alaska and composed of about 95 percent wasteland. It is a Muslim country, with 97 percent of its 4.2 million people being Berber and Arab. Rich in history—the site of Phoenicia and Carthage—its capital, Tripoli, has long had an important role as a transit point for people and goods from Africa to Europe.

Italy, as we have seen, occupied Libya from 1911 to the Second World War, when the country was placed under joint British/French control. It was not until 1952 that Libyan independence was finally achieved, and a federal monarchy under Sayyid Idris al-Sanusi was established.

Two powerful forces coincided in Libya during the 1960s. First was the influx of funds from the development of the oil industry. The second was the tide of Arab nationalism that swept the area as the tenets of Egyptian leader Jamal Abdel-Nasser took over the imagination of the Muslim world.

Nasserism was incompatible with the Sanusi government's pro-Western stand, and the citizens were furious when Libya declined to take a position on the 1967 Arab-Israeli war. Revolution was only a matter of time.

Libya's strongman

The revolution occurred in 1969 and was led by a 28-year-old captain named Mu'ammar Qaddafi. As had happened in Egypt in 1952, the Libyan revolt was a Free Officers movement, and once again a charismatic insider seized control.

Qaddafi embarked upon a career of political surprises, proposing union like an anxious suitor successively to Egypt and Sudan (1969), Syria (1970), Egypt and Syria (1971), Egypt (1972), and Tunisia (1974).

Qaddafi became more and more autocratic as he consolidated his power. In 1978 he began a terrorist movement to destroy opposition abroad. The terrible success of his efforts provoked the United States to respond with attacks on Tripoli and Benghazi in 1986, attacks which in the end

Libyan ruler Mu'ammar Qaddafi has controlled his nation's destiny since 1969.

probably enhanced Qaddafi's hold on his regime.

Libya did not join the coalition against Iraq, nor was it expected to. If Iraq wins, Qaddafi will certainly benefit. If Iraq loses, Qaddafi will probably remain in power until his own people decide to forcibly remove him.

Syria

The sudden alteration in U.S. relations with Syria has many parallels in history, perhaps the most pertinent being the change in U.S. and British attitudes toward the Soviet Union at the time of the German invasion in 1941. Before the invasion of Kuwait by Iraq, Syria and the United States were bitter enemies, divided on a variety of issues centering on Israel and Lebanon, but most clearly delineated by the 1983 attack on the Marine barracks in Beirut, Lebanon, by a Damascus-backed terrorist. But when Syria joined the UN coalition, practical politics dictated a new situation.

Hotbed of revolution

Few nations have had as turbulent a history as Syria, and almost none carry within themselves the seeds of anti-colonialism as Syria does. Natives of the country have long perceived their borders as artificial relics of the age of colonialism that interfered with the establishment of a larger, more cohesive Arab state. Fixated on that idea, yet divided by wide differences in sect, class, region, and ideology, united only by its Sunni Moslem heritage, the Syrian state became a petri dish of revolutionary cultures.

In 1963 the Ba'th party, as in Iraq, came to power in Syria and superimposed a unity from the top, nationalizing major sections of the economy and beginning widespread land reforms. The one-party military state that emerged

Syria has a large, well-equipped army, but one that reportedly is poorly trained. These soldiers ride a Soviet-built T-62 tank.

President Hafiz al Asad has controlled Syria since 1970. His rule has been ambitious and harsh.

proved itself incapable of a good military performance in the 1967 war against Israel, losing the indispensable Golan Heights. Partly as a result of this, power was seized in 1970 by Hafiz al Asad, who has become a major personality in not only Arab, but world political affairs.

Syria's long and bloody intervention in Lebanon, its continual state of war with Israel, and its brutal response to civil unrest among its own people (in 1982, Asad exterminated almost 10,000 of his own citizens involved in a fundamentalist religious uprising) have given the country and its leader an infamous reputation in the West—and the support of only Iran and Libya among the Arabs.

Syria now has one of the largest and best-equipped armies in the Middle East, although the force is, reportedly, poorly trained. The cost of maintaining these forces has placed a crippling burden upon the Syrian populace.

Syria's recent apparent reuniting of Beirut, possible only because the world's attention was diverted to the Gulf, made Syria the first nation to gain anything from the tragedy of war.

Quirk of logic

Yet Syria's presence with the Gulf Forces is an anomaly only an Arab logician could understand. Syria is as anti-U.S. as ever—America is still the "Great Satan"—and Syria is as pro-Iraqi as ever. It has taken issue with Iraq over Kuwait, not because it disapproves of the invasion, but because that invasion brought the United States to the area. Thus by a curious twist of logic, Syria is aligning with UN forces to force Iraq out of Kuwait, so that U.S. forces will leave the area. It is bizarre—but it is real.

If Iraq is defeated, then Syria will attempt to move into the vacuum thus created before its arch enemy Iran does, waving high the banner of Pan-Arabism. If Iraq wins, Syria can look forward to a brief honeymoon before its own long and bitter war with Saddam Hussein.

Turkey

All of the lands of the Middle East—and much more—once belonged to the Ottoman Empire, which after centuries of immense political power and cultural influence became "the sick man of Europe," and disintegrated at the end of the First World War. The empire left two totally different legacies, one to the states like Syria, Jordan, Saudi Arabia, and others that had composed it, and one to Turkey, where the capital, Constantinople, had been located.

Turkey looks to the West

Turkey, purified in the 1920s by the fires of military revolution led by Mustafa Kemal (later

Turkey's president, Turgut Ozal, aligned his nation with the anti-Iraq coalition, reflecting Turkey's long-standing linkage to the West.

called Kemal Ataturk, the "father" of his people) became revitalized. It retained the admirable bureaucratic efficiency of the old empire and sought to shape itself in the European mold, in part by de-emphasizing religion.

Turkey adroitly managed to stay out of the Second World War. Immediately after the war— on June 7, 1945—Russia presented Turkey with demands for territory and the right to establish bases in the Turkish straits. Turkey turned to the United States for support, and was subsequently included both in the Marshall Plan and, ultimately, NATO.

Turkey's relationship with the U.S. and the West has not been without bumps: The Turkish involvement in Cyprus began in the 1950s, and its forceful intervention there in 1974 severely damaged its relations with the U.S.

Stabilizing influence

In 1952, Turkey established formal diplomatic relations with Israel, a move that proved costly in terms of relations with Arab states. Now, under the leadership of President Turgut Ozal, Turkey has aligned itself with the coalition against Iraq, which has long menaced its borders. More than 120,000 Turkish troops now face Iraqi soldiers along the border.

If Iraq loses the Gulf War, Turkey's future importance as a stabilizing element will be immense in both the Middle East and in the Soviet Union, whose Muslim minorities pose an enormous threat to Soviet control. In time, Turkey may join the European Economic Community, fulfilling Kemal Ataturk's highest dreams.

Iran

The first Persian empire began in the sixth century B.C.—the next Persian empire may depend upon the results of the war in the Gulf.

A non-Arab but Moslem state, Iran is today a theocratic democracy, completely dominated by the clerics of the Islamic revolution. It is 95 percent Shi'a Muslim, and is at present enjoying welcome stability as the "enemy of its enemies," Iraq, is beset by the problems of the Gulf War.

Iran's relationships with the West started as most in the region did, with British commercial and military interests. Britain's First Sea Lord, Winston Churchill, wanted oil for his ships; Persia had the oil, and the Anglo-Persian Oil Company was formed to get it.

Exit Shah, enter Ayatollah

There was a great deal of fighting in Persia during the First World War, and the resulting

Following the 1979 overthrow of the Shah, power in Iran was seized by Ayatollah Rouhallah Khomeini, a Muslim fundamentalist.

turbulence allowed an illiterate Persian Cossack, Reza Shah Pahlavi, to lead a revolution that ultimately made him "shah-in-shah," or king of kings, establishing a reign that the U.S. would support through the 1979 fall of his grandson, Muhammad Reza Shah.

On April 1, 1979, the Islamic Republic of Iran was proclaimed by Ayatollah Rouhallah Khomeini. Unlike most colonel-engineered coups in the Middle East, this revolution was a genuine expression of social, religious, and political discontent. The Ayatollah immediately called for similar adherence to Muslim fundamentals throughout the Middle East.

Enemies or allies?

Iraqi leader Saddam Hussein was disturbed at this Shi'a initiative, saw that the Iranian military was disorganized, and launched his 1980 invasion of Iran. Yet after eight years of bloody conflict, after billions of dollars of expenditures and nearly as many words of invective, Iran's President Rafsanjani agreed to reestablish diplomatic relations with Iraq. This threatened the

Hashemi Rafsanjani, president of Iran, is undoubtedly poised to fill the power vacuum likely to result from an Iraqi collapse.

UN coalition that had arrayed itself against Saddam, and raised the possibility of everything from the smuggling of food to Iraq, to the threat of possible military cooperation between the two nations, including the harboring of Iraq's air force. The ideal solution for Iran would be for the war never to end, for the two great Satans to grind themselves into dust, which would then be swept away by the rising tide of Muslim fundamentalism.

Yemen Arab Republic (North Yemen)

This remote and desolate land—the ancient home of the Queen of Sheba—is largely supported by foreign aid and loyal Yemenis working abroad and sending home their remittances. Independence was acquired in 1918 as the troops of the ruined Ottoman Empire departed. The

In the Middle East, the traditional Arab lifestyle contrasts sharply with 20th century Western technology. The Persian Gulf war is marked by many such contrasts.

Saddam Hussein has been president of Iraq since 1979.

The Persian Gulf: a region in crisis

Labels on map:

Ankara • TURKEY • Erzurum • Tbilisi • Kir • Aleppo • SYRIA • Euphrates River • Mosul • Arbil • Tigris River • Bagh • CYPRUS • Beirut • LEBANON • Damascus • Karbala • IRAQ • Mediterranean Sea • ISRAEL • Tel Aviv • Golan Heights • Jerusalem • Amman • West Bank • Gaza Strip • JORDAN • Alexandria • Al Jawf • Suez Canal • Sinai Peninsula • Cairo • Tabuk • Hail • EGYPT • Nile River • Medina • SAUDI ARABIA • Aswan • Mecca • Jiddah • Lake Nasser • Red Sea • Port Sudan • SUDAN • Asmera • DJIBOUTI • ETHIOPIA • H

EGYPT	KUWAIT
Area: 386,650 square miles, about the size of Texas and New Mexico **Population:** 54,779,000 **Armed forces:** 320,000	**Area:** 6,880 square miles, slightly smaller than New Jersey **Population:** 1,967,000 **Pre-invasion armed forces:** 20,300

TURKEY	SYRIA	IRAQ	IRAN
Area: 301,381 square miles, almost twice the size of California **Population:** 56,549,000 **Armed forces:** 500,000	**Area:** 71,498 square miles, slightly larger than North Dakota **Population:** 12,210,000 **Armed forces:** 360,000	**Area:** 167,924 square miles, slightly larger than California **Population:** 17,610,000 **Armed forces:** 1 million	**Area:** 636,293 square miles, slightly larger than Alaska **Population:** 55,647,000 **Armed forces:** 604,500

SOURCE: World Almanac, Associated Press

SOVIET UNION

SOVIET UNION

Tashkent

Caspian Sea

Baku

AFGHANISTAN

Tehran

IRAN

Basra

Abadan

Shiraz

PAKISTAN

Kuwait City

KUWAIT

Persian Gulf

BAHRAIN

QATAR

OMAN

Riyadh

UNITED ARAB EMIRATES

Gulf of Oman

Muscat

OMAN

EUROPE

Area of map

AFRICA

ASIA

YEMEN

Gulf of Aden

Socotra (Yemen)

Arabian Sea

ANTARCTICA

SOMALIA

ISRAEL
Area: 7,847 square miles, about the size of New Jersey **Population:** 4,477,000 **Armed forces:** 141,000

JORDAN
Area: 37,737 square miles, slightly larger than Indiana **Population:** 3,031,000 **Armed forces:** 74,000

SAUDI ARABIA
Area: 839,996 square miles, almost the size of the United States east of the Mississippi **Population:** 12,678,000 **Armed forces:** 43,200

President George Bush has opposed Iraq's invasion of Kuwait from the beginning.

Iranian troops view a captured Iraqi tank. The Iran-Iraq War has made the Iraqi Army battle tough.

This Iraqi TV image claimed to show Iraqi troops withdrawing from Kuwait; there was no truth to the claim.

Sheik Jabir al-Ahmad al-Sabah, the emir of Kuwait, is the latest in a family line that has ruled Kuwait since 1756.

Among the first U.S. forces to reach Saudi Arabia during Operation Desert Shield were the 82nd Airborne Division.

Operation Desert Shield/Desert Storm has meant the heartbreak of separation for many families.

King Fahd of Saudi Arabia allowed U.S. and Allied troops into his country to counter Iraq's threat.

These newly arrived Allied soldiers train with gas masks to prepare for the threat of chemical warfare.

Iraqi troops parade in support of Saddam Hussein.

Members of the 82nd Airborne Division perform live-fire exercises with a Dragon antitank weapon.

The Persian Gulf war brought about a new twist: the proximity to the battlefront of women serving in U.S. armed forces.

Egyptian special forces are part of the Allied forces arrayed against Iraq.

President Hosni Mubarak of Egypt has been one of the staunchest Arab supporters of Allied efforts against Iraq.

New British Prime Minister John Major continued Margaret Thatcher's Gulf policies when he took power in the autumn of 1990.

A U.S. soldier shows Saudi Arabian marines how to operate an AT-4 84mm antitank weapon.

Many Iraqi men volunteered to join the Iraqi Popular Army in the wake of Allied deployment of forces along the Saudi-Kuwait border.

PLO leader Yasser Arafat came out strongly in favor of Saddam Hussein early in the Persian Gulf crisis.

On January 18, 1991, Hussein attempted to draw Israel into the war by launching Scud missile attacks at Tel Aviv.

In the opening weeks of the Persian Gulf war, Israeli Prime Minister Yitzhak Shamir did not allow his nation to retaliate despite several Iraqi missile attacks.

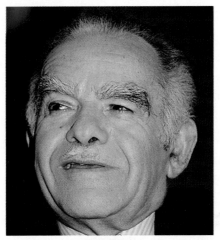

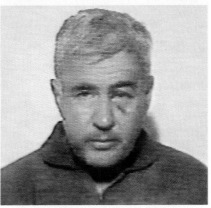

POW Marine Corps Chief Warrant Officer Guy Hunter as he appeared on Iraqi TV; this action was a violation of the Geneva Convention.

During the Persian Gulf war, King Hussein of Jordan has walked a narrow path between supporting Iraq and not alienating the West.

The unending Mideast strife that helped lead to the Persian Gulf war is exemplified by the violence in Lebanon.

On November 29, 1990, the United Nations approved the use of force after January 15, 1991, to oust Iraq from Kuwait.

Modern media brought the war to the world on a real-time basis until censorship and Saddam Hussein limited media access.

An oil refinery in Saudi Arabia burns after an Iraqi attack.

On January 19, 1991, protesters opposing the war in the Persian Gulf marched in Washington, D.C.

The world's largest oil slick, originating at the Sea Island Terminal just offshore of Kuwait, caused great harm to the Gulf's wildlife.

"The Bear" is one nickname for General Norman Schwarzkopf, commander of Allied forces in the Mideast. The sophistication of the weaponry at his disposal is almost incalculable.

Chairman of the Joint Chiefs of Staff General Colin Powell has been a steady, firm influence throughout the Gulf conflict.

F-15E Eagles flew many sorties in the first few days of Operation Desert Storm.

This Tornado belongs to 27 Squadron R.A.F. Marham.

The Iraqi Air Force flies MiG-21 Fishbed fighters similar to this one in Finnish colors.

The Soviet-made MiG-29 Fulcrum is Iraq's most advanced jet fighter.

A-10 Thunderbolt IIs are the best tank killers fielded by the U.S. Air Force.

The F-117A Stealth Fighter uses sophisticated technology to remain undetected by enemy radar.

French forces have been participating in Allied efforts using their Mirage 2000 fighters.

B-52 Stratofortress bombers have pounded Republican Guard positions continually.

This AH-64 Apache helicopter fires a Hellfire missile during a training exercise.

The Harpoon antiship missile is so versatile that it can be launched from aircraft, ships, or submarines.

Although Iraq has many more tanks at its disposal than the Allies, the American M-1 Abrams MBT is powerful enough to dominate the battlefield.

The U.S. Army uses the M113 Armored Personnel Carrier to move infantry during ground operations.

This may look like a Jeep but it is actually an HMMWV, the U.S. Army's replacement for the venerable Jeep.

Allied forces counter Iraqi superiority in artillery with the M109 155mm Self-propelled Howitzer.

The Multiple Launch Rocket System can blanket a large area with thousands of bomblets.

The Patriot missile system has proved more than a match for aging, Soviet-made Scud missiles.

Several Nimitz-class aircraft carriers are stationed in the Mideast during this conflict.

The Wisconsin *(BB 64) is one of two U.S. Iowa-class battleships on duty in the Persian Gulf.*

Tarawa-*class Amphibious Assault Ships* play a major role in any Marine amphibious landing.

The Tomahawk cruise missile has given a new lease on life to Iowa-class battleships.

Yemeni president Ali Abdullah Saleh (left) meets with King Fahd of Saudi Arabia.

agricultural areas formerly used for crops are now devoted largely to qat, a mild narcotic chewed incessantly by native Yeminis. Only in the last few years has oil production begun in the area.

Yet despite its isolation and its comparative poverty—life expectancy of the people is only about 48 years—Yemen occupies a strategic location at the mouth of the Red Sea, and has thus been the focus of interest of Italy, Great Britain, and Turkey over the years, and of war with Saudi Arabia, which occupied it in 1934.

Yemen became a client of Nasser's Egypt, and began relying heavily on Soviet support. In 1962 a revolution resulted in the establishment of North Yemen as the Yemen Arab Republic.

Civil wars

The years after the revolution were beset by civil wars as republicans battled dynastic royalists. Like Spain in 1937, foreign armies came to fight—Egyptian for the republicans, Saudi Arabian for the royalists.

A coalition government was established in 1970, but there was continuous political conflict until mid-1982. Since then the Yemen Arab Republic tried to follow a middle course in Arab politics, fighting only with its severed half, South Yemen (the People's Republic of Yemen). In 1991, the Yemen Arab Republic merged with South Yemen.

The Gulf War's embargo is having a devastating effect on the already suffering Yemeni economy. Now in union with its southern brother, Yemen, despite its isolation, needs peace in the Gulf.

South Yemen (People's Republic of Yemen)

South Yemen is one of the poorest of the Arab countries, with few natural resources, a scattered population of just over two million, and a stagnant economy that imports five times the amount of its exports. Recent oil discoveries may improve this situation.

Its capital, Aden, has long been a flourishing port, and originally was one of Great Britain's key communications links with its empire. After the First World War, the area, called "South Arabia," became a colony ruled by Great Britain, but with a great deal of freedom allowed the tribal leaders of the interior.

After the revolution of 1962 that ripped the nation in two, South Yemen suffered a protracted civil war that was ultimately won by the National Liberation Front. In 1967, the independence of South Yemen was proclaimed.

Independence woes

Independence brought problems: The British no longer subsidized the government, and the Arab-Israeli war had closed the Suez Canal, denying Aden its customary maritime traffic. South Yemen drifted more and more into the Soviet orbit, relying heavily on Eastern Bloc countries for aid, a policy without much future.

At a time when communism has failed in countries with enormous resources, the People's Republic of Yemen is continuing to strive to manage its impoverished economy in a truly socialistic manner. The nation's 1991 merger with North Yemen may improve the economic picture.

The results of the war in the Gulf will probably have little consequence to South Yemen except to further decrease Eastern-Bloc aid. If Iraq wins, and takes Saudi Arabia, it may well extend its "benevolence" to South Yemen. An Iraqi loss probably won't affect this sad but valiant state.

Japan

A recent best seller in Japan bore the message that "Japan can say no."

Japan has certainly said no to its chance to begin flexing superpower muscles by decisive intervention in the Gulf War, a conflict in which it has a stake far greater than even the United States. Japan must import more than 99 percent of its crude oil; about 70 percent of its total needs

Japanese prime minister Toshiki Kaifu heads one of the world's wealthiest—and most oil-dependent—nations, yet was slow to give the Gulf coalition appropriate monetary support.

comes from the Middle East. An interruption of the supply or a significant increase in price would have an enormous, adverse effect upon the Japanese economy.

Japan originally pledged one billion dollars to offset the cost of the Gulf War—an amount roughly comparable to the dimes that John D. Rockefeller used to hand out to beggars on the street. Indignant members of the U.S. House of Representatives reacted to Japan's offer by passing a bill calling for the removal of 50,000 American troops from Japan; Tokyo responded by raising the ante to four billion dollars. Of that amount, two billion dollars is to go to the United States to offset the cost of the war (an amount that would pay for less than four days' expenditures), and two billion dollars to impoverished Middle Eastern countries.

Economic realities

While the Japanese claim that constitutional requirements and national sentiment prevent them from overt military gestures, their response to date has seemed both cynical and lacking in self-interest. The monstrous growth of the Japanese economy is already showing signs of slackening, making it unwise for Japan to fail to support the coalition in the Gulf—a coalition composed of Japan's greatest trading partners. The Gulf War has in fact become a two-edged sword for Japan, on the one hand threatening to increase oil prices to the point that the Japanese economy is destroyed, and on the other destroying the economies of Japan's trading partners. The Gulf situation is one to which Japan *cannot* say no—it is clearly in Japan's own interest to be more forthcoming with military and financial aid. If it is not, it may stand to lose the most of any nation.

Lebanon

After years of domination by the Ottoman Empire, the state of Lebanon fell under the post-World War I French Mandate that also extended to Syria. Smaller than the state of Connecticut, with a population of over three million, Lebanon is a nation blessed by nature and cursed by politics. Left untroubled, Lebanon has the resources to become an agricultural, industrial, and cultural center of the Middle East.

Although its population is 93 percent Arab and six percent Armenian, its religions are divided on the basis of 75 percent Muslim and 25 percent Christian. There are 17 recognized religious sects in Lebanon, each one contributing to the continuing strife that rends the country.

Lebanon received full independence in 1943, and during the initial post-war period closely aligned itself with U.S. policies, which caused

The fighting stance of this Shiite militiaman in Beirut sums up the agony of Lebanon.

difficulties with its two most powerful neighbors—Syria and Egypt.

Lebanon crumbles

The Arab-Israeli war of 1967 proved to be disastrous for Lebanon, as Palestinian guerrilla forces set up operations in the country; the Palestine Liberation Organization soon began to increase its influence there. Israeli military forces began retaliatory strikes against PLO forces within Lebanon, which accelerated the process of the destabilization of the Lebanese government.

Civil war broke out in 1975, and Syria intervened, taking action against Palestinians and Lebanese factions alike. Israel invaded the country in 1977 and again in 1981, in an effort to suppress the activities of PLO guerrillas. The UN multi-national force that was supposed to police

President Sheikh Zayed bin Suktan al Nahyan heads the government of the terrifically wealthy United Arab Emirates.

Lebanon withdrew in 1984, after devastating terrorist attacks on the U.S. embassy and on the American and French barracks.

A no-win situation

As noted earlier, Syria now dominates Lebanon politics. In the meantime, the country has been destroyed, thousands have been killed, the economy is collapsing—and nothing has changed. Whether Iraq wins or loses the Gulf War will probably have no effect on the sad train of events in Lebanon.

United Arab Emirates

The United Arab Emirates consists of a federation of seven states. Its population of just over two million people enjoys one of the world's highest per capita incomes, thanks to the immense oil and natural gas reserves of the region.

The UAE could scarcely be more importantly located in strategic terms, lying on both sides of

Despite its wealth, the UAE fields a modest military. Here, UAE volunteers assemble for duty.

the Straits of Hormuz, and with shorelines within the Persian Gulf and the Gulf of Oman.

Less than 20 percent of the UAE population are citizens—fully 50 percent are South East Asian laborers, mostly Indian and Pakistani, who toil in the nation's oil fields. Not surprisingly, trade unions are illegal, and the Emirian segment of the population, descendants of the Qawasim and Bani Yas tribes that have ruled the area for 6,000 years, live very well.

Known as the Trucial States until 1971 by reason of their many treaties with Great Britain, the United Arab Emirates came into being as a result of England's decision to liquidate its military holdings in the Middle East. The new federation was founded in 1971, in an effort to protect the development of the oil fields discovered in 1958.

The power of wealth

Oil revenues began to soar in 1974, and it is probably only the fact that the wealth has

Khalifa bin Hamad al-Thani holds absolute power in tiny but oil-rich Qatar. The Thani family has ruled Qatar for more than 70 years.

become so incalculable that the UAE has hung together. There is no loyalty except to tribe, boundaries are ill-defined, and power is typically transferred by palace coup. If Iraq wins the war, the UAE will be a plum ripe for plucking. If Iraq loses, the Emirians will continue to live lives of unbelievable luxury, shielded from the poverty that characterizes so much of the Middle East.

Qatar

Tiny Qatar protrudes into the Persian Gulf like a wart from the finger of the Arabian peninsula. This tiny land, so inhospitable that its water must come from desalinization plants, has proven oil reserves of 3.3 billion barrels, giving it a per capita income of $17,000—one of the highest in the world.

Ties that bind

The Thani family dominated the region when Britain came to control most of the Gulf at the close of the First World War. In 1971, when Qatar became an independent Gulf state, the Thani family continued to rule.

The Chief of State and Head of Government, Amir and Prime Minister Khalifa bin Hamad al-Thani, holds absolute power in the kingdom—there are no political parties, no elections, nothing but advice from a council of ministers—all members of the Thani family.

If Iraq should win the Gulf War, Qatar is a strong candidate to become Iraq's twenty-first province, after Saudi Arabia becomes the twentieth.

Morocco

Like Libya, Morocco is part of the *jazirat al-maghrib* (islands of the west), a self-contained region bounded on the east and south by desert, on the north by the Mediterranean Sea, and on the west by the Atlantic Ocean.

Morocco's Sunni Muslim population is 99 percent Berber-Arab, and the nation's climate is perhaps the best of all the Arab states, benefiting from rainfall originating in both the Atlantic and Mediterranean areas. Morocco also has a long history of excellent tribal administration, and preserved its independence until it was occupied by France and Spain in 1912.

The French treated Morocco in a considerably more civilized manner than they had Algeria, while the Spanish were locked into a seemingly unending war with Morocco's Riffian tribes. It was in this conflict that General Francisco Franco first made a name for himself.

Morocco's King Hassan II has provided his nation with brave, thoughtful rule since ascending to the throne in 1961.

The Moroccan desire for independence was heightened when American troops occupied the country in 1942 and dismissed the Vichy French government. When the Algerian rebellion broke out in 1954, France realized that it had to make a sacrifice to try to save the more important Algeria, so independence was granted to Morocco in 1956. A year later, the former Sultan of Morocco became King. The present King Hassan II acceded to the throne in 1961.

Hassan charts his course

The intervening years have been turbulent, and King Hassan II has demonstrated both political acumen and personal bravery in steering a course through attempted revolution and aggression by both Algeria and Libya, although relations have improved with the latter country.

Morocco's participation in the United Nations coalition against Iraq is a tribute to King Hassan II's larger view of Morocco's role in the world, particularly in view of Libya's implicit support of the Iraqis.

Bahrain

Bahrain is a tiny archipelago of 30 islands with a land mass about three times as large as Washington D.C. Britain gained control of Bahrain in 1820. During the interval of British rule, there were occasional claims made on the island by Iran, but in 1971 independence was granted by Great Britain. Iran did not contest the issue at the time, but during the 1980s again began to assert that Bahrain was rightfully Iranian.

Oil, communications, and finance

Like the other members of the Gulf Cooperation Council (GCC), Bahrain's economy is now heavily dependent upon the oil industry, which has its roots in discoveries made in the mid-1930s. Emphasis has shifted from crude oil to refined products, however, as Bahrainian reserves have been depleted.

Perhaps more importantly, while Bahrain continues to be an important port facility, it has come to be one of the most important communications and banking centers in the world; more than 70 offshore Bahrainian banks are in operation. The country also has a burgeoning industrial capacity, which has helped to diversify the economy.

Bahrain's continued existence undoubtedly depends upon the maintenance of the status quo in the Middle East. If Iraq becomes a regional superpower, Bahrain will lose its independent identity, for it is unlikely that Saddam Hussein would not covet the nation's wealth.

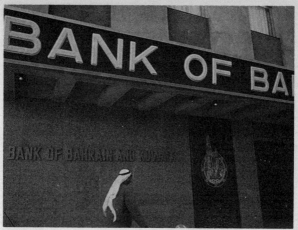

Bahrain is a world leader in banking and finance. More than 70 offshore Bahrainian banks are in operation.

Pakistan

While not part of the Middle East, Pakistan's huge and growing population (nearly 115 million) of intensely devout Muslims could be a critical factor in the ignition of a holy war.

As a very poor Third World country, Pakistan is beset with unusual problems. It has tremendous internal political difficulties, as the recent dismissal of Prime Minister Benazir Bhutto indicated. The government is heavily in debt, and almost completely dependent upon foreign aid to survive.

At the same time, it is necessary for Pakistan to support a huge military establishment because of the nation's continuing armed conflicts with India. Pakistan has also been providing for the outpouring of refugees from

Prime Minister Mohammad Nawaz Sharif of Pakistan struggles with a crippled economy and his people's unhappiness with Pakistan's participation in the Allied coalition.

Afghanistan—more than four million, all of whom must be fed and sheltered.

Dangerous dissent

There is a strong Pakistani sense of identity with the Pan-Arab cause, and the populace is becoming increasingly vociferous in its support for Saddam Hussein, particularly in view of the Pakistani government's decision to join the Allied coalition and dispatch 5,000 troops to the Gulf. In the eyes of many Pakistanis, these troops have been wrongly sent to "fight their Arab brothers." While the Pakistani government has contained popular dissent so far, the importance of the Muslim influence on Pakistan and other nations in the world—particularly in Indonesia—should not be underestimated.

Somewhat curiously, of all the expressions of support for either the UN forces or Iraq, that of the Pakistani government is the most unalloyed by self-interest. Indeed, by choosing to support the Allies, the government of Pakistan may only have stirred up a hornet's nest in its own back yard.

Oman

The Sultanate of Oman is a small, hot, and generally arid nation that has been home to human beings since antiquity—for at least 10,000 years. More than 90 percent of the approximately 1.4 million people who now make up its population live in rural areas. As with other Middle Eastern nations, Oman's economy is heavily dependent upon oil.

Arabs first settled in Oman in the 9th century, B.C.; tribal warfare characterized much of the nation's early history. Islam was adopted in the 7th century, A.D. and Oman was subsequently dominated by Islamic imams (spiritual leaders).

Pro-West

Internal strife between Omani tribes and the ruling dynasties continued until 1959, when the last imam was deposed. British influence was formalized in a 1951 treaty, and Oman has retained a pro-West stance. Oman joined the Arab League and the United Nations in 1971.

As part of the coalition allied against Iraq, Oman brings a well-trained army and a recent history of close ties to Great Britain and the United States. Although Oman's oil reserves are not as great as those in other Middle Eastern nations, Oman would nonetheless tempt Saddam Hussein in the event of the Iraqi dictator's ascendance to control of the region.

WEAPONS
OF THE GULF WAR

Air Weaponry

The F-15 Eagle is part of the Allied air force.

Fighters, attack jets, bombers, reconnaissance planes, helicopters. All of these were brought to bear by the United States in the Desert Storm campaign against Iraq. Firmly anchored by these awesome fighting machines, the United Nations established air-superiority with blinding speed and intensity not seen since the Middle East Six Day War of 1967. Every element of the UN forces—land-based and seaborne—functioned within a computer-like war plan that slashed through essential Iraqi command and control installations like a knife though a jugular vein.

The mission

The initial passive resistance of the Iraqi air forces was surprising, permitting UN forces to concentrate on Iraq's greatest threat: the fixed and mobile Scud missile launchers. The fixed units were attacked at the outset, but the mobile units by their very nature presented a difficult target.

United States air power faced its toughest challenge when it turned its attention to Iraqi troops, artillery, and tanks—all entrenched in desert dug-outs. There, a new chapter in combat history will be written: massive tonnages of bombs dropped by B-52s, augmented by precision strikes with smart bombs. American air power had arrived.

F-14 Tomcat
Grumman F-14 Tomcat

The F-14 is the U.S. Navy's most formidable fighter.

The F-14 Tomcat was designed as a fleet air-defense interceptor capable of serving into the 21st century. It is the latest in a long line of Grumman "carrier cats" that date back to before World War II. Designed in the late 1960s, it was determined early on that the F-14 would be a "cat"; and since the man behind the project was Admiral Tom Connelly, then Deputy Chief of Naval Operations for Air, the new airplane was dubbed Tom's Cat. The Tomcat first flew in 1970; today, nearly 400 Tomcats are operational on U.S. Navy carriers.

Combat-tested

The F-14 was blooded in combat prior to Operation Desert Storm. On August 19, 1981, two Navy F-14 crews shot down two Libyan Su-22 fighters over the Gulf of Sidra in the Mediterranean Sea when the Libyan warplanes made threatening moves toward the aircraft carrier *Nimitz*; and on January 4, 1989, two F-14 crews from the carrier *John F. Kennedy* downed a pair of Libyan MiG-23s in the same area.

The F-14 has variable-geometry wings that can change shape in flight to match speed and altitude requirements. Wingspan is 64 feet unswept, and 38 feet swept back. The Tomcat is 16 feet high, 62 feet long, and weighs 74,349 pounds. Two General Electric F110-GE-400 Turbofans, each with 28,500 pounds of thrust, propel the F-14 at a maximum speed of 1,734 miles per hour. Maximum range is 2,000 miles; service ceiling is 50,000 feet.

The Tomcat carries a crew of two, a pilot and a backseater who operates the complex offensive radar and weapons systems. It is armed with a 20 millimeter cannon, as well as an assortment of guided missiles such as the AIM-9 Sidewinder and AIM-54 Phoenix air-to-air missiles. The Phoenix missile was designed especially for use by the F-14.

F-15 Eagle
McDonnell Douglas F-15 Eagle—United States

The F-15 Eagle is comparable to the F-14 Tomcat in that it represents the leading edge of fighter

The F-15 may be the best fighter in the world.

technology as defined by the mission requirements of the U.S. Air Force. Widely regarded as
the best air-superiority fighter in the world, the
F-15 demonstrated its superior capabilities
above Lebanon's Bekaa valley in June 1982,
when Israeli F-15s downed 58 Soviet-built Syrian fighters at no loss to themselves.

The best of everything

The multi-role capability of the F-15 makes it
one of the most versatile and cost-effective fighters in history. The plane was designed to take
everything that had been learned in air-to-air
combat in Vietnam, add the best that emerging
electronics technology had to offer, and build the
best possible fighter to fulfill the Air Force mission. The first Eagles flew in July 1972, and the
first F-15As entered squadron service four years
later. The F-15C was introduced in 1979. By the
early 1980s, Eagles had already begun to replace

the F-4 Phantoms as the Air Force's first-line fighters. In 1987, the Air Force began taking deliveries of the F-15E, a long-range two-seat fighter-bomber based on the F-15D.

The F-15 has wingspan of 43 feet, and is 64 feet long and 19 feet high. The 68,000-pound Eagle can attain a maximum speed in excess of Mach 2.5 through the use of two Pratt and Whitney F100-PW-100 turbofan engines, each providing 23,830 pounds of thrust. Range is 3,570 miles, service ceiling is 60,000 feet, maximum weight at take-off is 68,000 pounds. The Eagle's armament includes a 20 millimeter cannon, as well as AIM-7 Sparrow, AIM-9 Sidewinder, and AMRAAM air-to-air missiles.

In addition to the United States, the F-15 is also in service in the Israeli and Saudi Arabian Air Forces. On January 24, 1991, a Saudi F-15 pilot (identified only as "Captain Ayedh") used air-to-air missiles to down two Iraqi F-1 Mirages while the latter were attempting to attack British warships in the gulf with Exocet antiship missiles.

F-16 Fighting Falcon
General Dynamics
F-16 Fighting Falcon—
United States

The F-16 Fighting Falcon saw action against Iraq prior to Desert Storm when, in June 1981, Israeli F-16 fighter-bombers were used to attack and destroy the Iraqi nuclear plant at Osirak.

The F-16 Fighting Falcon was named after the mascot of the U.S. Air Force Academy in Col-

Swift and agile: the F-16 Fighting Falcon.

orado Springs, Colorado. The idea behind the
F-16 was to build a large number of lightweight,
low-cost fighters to augment the squadrons of
larger, more expensive F-15s. Although the primary F-16 assembly line is at the General
Dynamics plant in Fort Worth, Texas, the aircraft is also produced by factories in Belgium
and the Netherlands. The first F-16 squadron
was activated by the U.S. Air Force in 1979.
Since then, F-16s have been adapted for service
in a number of NATO countries as well as Israel.

The Electric Jet

The F-16 is a single-seat aircraft. Swift and
agile yet capable of carrying heavy bomb loads, it
may serve as an interceptor or fighter-bomber.
The Fighting Falcon is a fly-by-wire aircraft,
meaning that its control services (flaps, rudder,
etc.) are operated by a computerized network of
electric motors rather than hydraulics. Hence,
the F-16's nickname, the Electric Jet.

The F-16C is easy to service and has one of the lowest turn-around times in the Desert Storm theater; changing either one of the Pratt and Whitney F100-PE-220 turbofan engines (General Electric F110-GE-100 turbofans on some models) takes about 30 minutes. The F-16's engines each provide 25,000 pounds of thrust, enabling the aircraft to achieve Mach 2 speeds. The Fighting Falcon has a 31-foot wingspan, and is 49 feet high and 17 feet long; maximum take-off weight is 42,300 pounds. The aircraft's service ceiling is 50,000 feet, and maximum range is 2,415 miles.

The F-16 may be armed with AIM-9 Sidewinder and AIM-120 AMRAAM air-to-air missiles, and/or conventional and nuclear bombs, the AGM-85 Maverick missile, and the AGM-45 Shrike and AGM-88 HARM antiradar missiles. The F-16 is also armed with a 20 mm cannon.

F/A-18 Hornet
McDonnell Douglas F/A-18 Hornet— United States

The F/A-18 Hornet evolved from the Northrop YF-17, which was rejected by the Air Force in favor of the YF-16. The Hornet is the U.S. Navy's close-in air-superiority fighter, and is charged with the task of defending aircraft carrier task forces. The Marine Corps also uses the Hornet as an attack aircraft in support of ground forces. Whether used by the Navy or Marine Corps, the Hornet is the same plane; the "F" and "A" designations indicate that it may be employed as both an interceptor and a fighter-bomber.

The F/A-18 Hornet defends aircraft carrier task forces.

Relatively small

The first F/A-18 Hornet flew in November of 1978, but did not officially enter service until 1983. The Hornet is a relatively small aircraft weighing 36,710 pounds and measuring 56 feet in length, 15 feet in height, and 37 feet across the wings. Two General Electric F404-GE-400 turbofan engines each provide 16,000 pounds of thrust for a top speed of 1,190 miles per hour. Maximum range for the Hornet is 2,303 miles; service ceiling is 50,000 feet.

The Hornet's armament includes a 20 millimeter cannon mounted on the top center of its nose. In its fighter configuration, the Hornet carries AIM-9 Sidewinder air-to-air missiles on wingtip racks; other weapons, such as the AIM-7 Sparrow missile, are carried underwing. For attack/fighter-bomber missions, the F/A-18's armorer can arm the aircraft with conventional or nuclear bombs, AGM-88 HARM antiradar missiles, AGM-65 Maverick air-to-ground missiles, AGM-109 Harpoon missiles, and SLAM air-to-ground missiles.

In addition to the single-seat Hornet, the Navy has procured a two-seat variant (F/A-18C/D), which is designed to provide all-weather/night attack capabilities. The F/A-18 Hornet is also employed in the Desert Storm offensive by the Canadian Air Force under the designation CF-18.

Mirage F-1
Dassault-Breguet Mirage F-1C—Iraq

The Mirage F-1 is a single-seat, all-weather, all-altitude interceptor. Although it has been superseded in the French Air Force by the Mirage 2000, it remains an integral part of the Iraqi combat aviation arm, which had about 94 F-1s prior to the Operation Desert Storm offensive.

The Dassault-Breguet aircraft company flew its first F-1 Mirage in January of 1967. The F-1C was the first major variant adopted by the French Air Force. The C model first flew in February 1973, and more than 210 are currently in service.

Exocet antiship missiles

The F-1C can be equipped with two 30 millimeter single-barrel cannons and two air-to-air missiles on wingtip hard points. The aircraft can

The Mirage F-1 is capable but obsolete.

also carry up to 8,818 pounds of bombs and other missiles on seven hard point pylons on the fuse-lage and under the wings. Two Iraqi F-1s armed with Exocet antiship missiles were used to attack allied warships in the Persian Gulf on January 24, 1991. Both planes were shot down by a single F-15 Eagle from the Saudi Arabian Air force.

Another F-1 variant is the F-1A, a ground-attack bomber that originally lacked the sophis-ticated radar and navigational aids found on the U.S. F-111 or the British Tornado. Most F-1As have since been retrofitted with a head-up-dis-play and a multifunction radar highly resistant to electronic countermeasures. The F-1B is a two-seat trainer that is quite similar to the F-1C, but the two 30mm cannons have been omitted. If the F-1B were pressed into operational use, it could be fitted with external gun pods.

The Mirage F-1C has a wingspan of 32 feet with missiles, and is 50 feet long and 14 feet high. Maximum take-off weight is 35,715 pounds, maximum range is 2,050 miles, and service ceiling is 65,600 feet. One SNECMA Atar 9K-50 turbojet engine provides a top speed of Mach 2.2.

Although an excellent multi-role fighter, the Mirage F-1 has been rendered obsolete by the outstanding Mirage 2000. And as events in Operation Desert Storm have proved, it is no match for more modern aircraft like the F-15 Eagle.

Mirage 2000
Dassault-Breguet Mirage 2000—France

In December 1975, the French government approved the development of a new delta-wing fighter aircraft to be called the Mirage 2000. This aircraft flew for the first time on March 10, 1978. The first French Air Force squadron equipped with the 2000-series fighter became operational in July 1984.

The Mirage 2000's delta wing increases lifting capacity and greatly improves the aircraft's low-speed, low-altitude performance—except in respect to fuel consumption rates, which are relatively high. The delta wing also facilitates high-speed handling at high altitudes.

Fly-by-wire
Control is maintained by a computer-operated fly-by-wire system. This system automatically

The Mirage 2000 is a successful interceptor.

adjusts aerodynamic control surfaces and engine output to keep the aircraft stable.

The Mirage 2000 has a wingspan of 30 feet, is 47 feet long and 17 feet high. Maximum take-off weight is 37,480 pounds; maximum range is 1,118 miles, and service ceiling is 59,000 feet. The aircraft is powered by one SNECMA M53-P2 turbofan engine providing 21,385 pounds of thrust to achieve a top speed of Mach 2.26.

The Mirage 2000 has nine hard point pylons (four under the wings, five under the fuselage) that can carry up to 13,890 pounds of ordnance. Weapons include air-to-air and other missiles, rockets, and various bombs. The aircraft is also equipped with two 30 millimeter cannons built into the fuselage.

Although its performance as a low-altitude strike-fighter is less than desired, the Mirage 2000 has proved to be an extremely successful interceptor. In addition to the French Air Forces, the Mirage 2000 flies with the air forces of Egypt, Greece, India, Jordan, Peru, and the United Arab Emirates.

MiG-21 MF Fishbed
Mikoyan-Gurevich MiG-21 Fishbed — Iraq

No-frills fighter: the MiG-21 Fishbed.

The MiG-21, NATO code-named Fishbed, has been widely used in the Soviet Air Force and exported to more than 34 nations, including Iraq. Iraq also uses a MiG-21 variant manufactured in the People's Republic of China, where it is designated the J-7. Iraq has approximately 150 MiG-21s and another 40 of the J-7 variant.

Originally designed as a low-altitude air-superiority fighter, later versions of the MiG-21 added a light strike capability. The first production model, the MiG-21F, entered service in the Soviet Air Force in 1959 as a clear-weather, day-only fighter interceptor.

No-frills fighter

In essence, the MiG-21 is a no-frills, highly maneuverable air-superiority fighter that can be adapted for the ground-attack role. It is quite small, and its combat radius is limited by its small internal fuel capacity. Hard points on the wings carry a range of air-to-air missiles; air-to-ground missiles and bombs are used in a light strike role. The MiG-21 was originally designed to carry two 30 millimeter NR-30 cannons, but the left gun had to be removed to meet weight restrictions and to provide room for avionics.

The MiG-21MF Fishbed-J has a wingspan of 24 feet, and is 52 feet long and 14 feet high. Its maximum take-off weight is 20,725 pounds. One Tumansky R-13-300 turbojet engine provides 14,550 pounds of thrust, and powers the aircraft at a Mach 2.1 top speed. Maximum range is 1,118 miles, and service ceiling is 50,000 feet.

The model seen most often in non-Soviet air forces is the MiG-21bis. This version is far more powerful than the original MiG-21, and carries a heavier armament.

MiG-29 Fulcrum
Mikoyan-Gurevich MiG-29 Fulcrum—Iraq

The MiG-29, NATO code-named Fulcrum, is perhaps the Soviet Union's most capable fighter

The MiG-29 is a world-class fighter interceptor.

interceptor and most agile aircraft.

It was originally designed as an air-superiority fighter, but after further development, the ground-attack role was added. The aircraft first flew in the early 1980s and was operational with Soviet fighter squadrons by 1985.

The MiG-29 is a single-seat aircraft, although the Fulcrum B variant has two seats for the training role. In the fighter role, the MiG-29 is armed with one 30 millimeter multibarrel cannon in the left wing. On three pylons under each wing it also carries AA-10 air-to-air missiles for long-range and AA-11 missiles for short-range work. In the attack mode, the aircraft can also carry the three sizes of air-to-ground rockets used by Soviet forces (240mm, 80mm, and 57mm), as well as a variety of gravity bombs.

Look-down/shoot-down radar

The MiG-29 Fulcrum has a pulse-doppler look-down/shoot-down radar that can identify enemy aircraft flying below it, and then direct air-to-air missiles to the enemy aircraft. It is thought that this radar is not able to track an enemy aircraft while searching for additional threats.

The Fulcrum is powered by two Tumansky RD-33 turbofan engines, each providing 18,300 pounds of thrust to attain a top speed of Mach 2.3. The aircraft is 57 feet long, 15 feet high, and 38 feet across the wings; maximum take-off weight range is 39,000 pounds and 1,300 miles, respectively; service ceiling is 56,000 feet.

The MiG-29 is certain to remain in frontline service with the Soviet Union well into the next century. In addition to Iraq, which has about 30 MiG-29s, Fulcrums are flown by the air forces of various other nations allied with the Soviet Union.

A-6 Intruder
Grumman A-6 Intruder — United States

The A-6 is an old soldier from the Vietnam War.

The A-6 Intruder is a versatile two-seat, medium-attack aircraft with all-weather, day-night attack capabilities. All A-6 variants feature a side-by-side seating arrangement typical of much larger planes. The pilot occupies the left seat, while the weapons system operator/navigator occupies the seat on the right.

Laser-guided

The first A-6 variant was flown in 1960. The most numerous variant is the A-6E, which was introduced in 1970. All A-6Es have since been converted into the A-6E/TRAM (Target Recognition and Attack Multisensor). TRAM's electronics, which are carried in a turret located under the nose, are designed for infrared- and laser-guided weapons. The TRAM system on the A-6E can illuminate a target with a laser while a second A-6E launches weapons against it, using the first A-6E's laser reflection to guide the weapons.

The A-6E can also be armed with nuclear bombs, conventional "iron" bombs, AGM-84 Harpoon antiship missiles, and SLAM air-to-ground missiles. The maximum combined load of ordnance and drop tanks is 18,000 pounds. The A-6E has a 53-foot wingspan, weighs 60,400 pounds, and is 55 feet long and 16 feet high. Two Pratt and Whitney J52-P-8B turbojet engines each provide 9,300 pounds of thrust. Top speed is 648 miles per hour; maximum range is 2,740 miles; service ceiling is 42,400 feet.

The EA-6B Prowler is an electronic warfare Intruder variant with a crew of four. In order to accommodate the additional two crew members (who operate electronic countermeasures hardware), the Prowler is five feet longer than the Intruder. Each Prowler is equipped to carry two AGM-88A HARM antiradar missiles.

AV-8B Harrier II
McDonnell Douglas AV-8B Harrier II—United States

The remarkable Harrier can take off and land vertically.

The AV-8B Harrier II is an outgrowth of a design pioneered by the Hawker aircraft company in Britain. After its British debut in the late 1960s, this vertical take-off and landing (VTOL) aircraft attracted the attention of the U.S. Marine Corps, which was interested in using Harriers for close air support of amphibious operations. The Marines ordered 110 Harriers, which entered service in 1971 as the AV-8A Harrier.

In 1975, McDonnell Douglas developed an improved Harrier with a larger wing that nearly doubled the aircraft's range and payload. By 1982, a joint manufacturing agreement had been worked out between British Aerospace (which had absorbed Hawker) and McDonnell Douglas whereby the American company would produce the up-rated VTOL aircraft designating it AV-8B Harrier II.

The AV-8B Harrier II has a wingspan of 30 feet, a maximum take-off weight of 29,750 pounds, and is 46 feet long and 12 feet high. Maximum range and top speed are 2,015 miles and 683 miles per hour, respectively; service ceiling is 50,000 feet. The aircraft is powered by one Rolls-Royce F402-RR-402 turbojet engine delivering 21,500 pounds of thrust. The Harrier can be armed with a 25 millimeter cannon, a four-ton bomb load, or a variety of guided air-to-ground munitions, as well as the AIM-9L Sidewinder air-to-air missile.

Falklands ace

During the 1982 Falkland Islands War, Royal Navy Harriers flew more than 2,000 attack missions against Argentinean targets. In the process, they managed to shoot down 20 enemy aircraft without a single loss. Like their British counterparts, today's U.S. Marine Corps AV-8B Harrier pilots are trained to fly in the interceptor and ground attack roles while supporting joint Navy/Marine amphibious operations.

A-10 Thunderbolt II
Fairchild Republic A-10 Thunderbolt II— United States

Nobody calls the A-10 the Thunderbolt. Even its most ardent proponents call it the Warthog. Ugly and misshapen though it may be, however, it is nonetheless the deadliest ground-attack aircraft in any nation's air force.

The A-10 is admired by its pilots, feared by its enemies.

Tank buster

The first A-10 variant was flown in 1972 and entered Air Force service shortly thereafter as the A-10A. The single-seat A-10 is especially effective as a "tank-busting" aircraft. Its main armament is a formidable GAU-8 Avenger 30 millimeter rotary cannon with 1,200 rounds. This seven-barrel weapon fires high-velocity slugs with depleted uranium tips. Depleted uranium, which is not radioactive, is heavier than lead or steel and is capable of penetrating heavy tank armor.

In addition to the Avenger cannon, the A-10 can carry eight tons of air-to-ground munitions, including "iron" bombs, "smart" bombs, cluster bombs, AGM-65 air-to-ground Maverick missiles, and AIM-9 Sidewinder air-to-air missiles. Electronic countermeasures equipment can also be carried on the A-10's eight underwing pylons.

The A-10A has a wingspan of 58 feet, and is 53 feet long and 14 feet high. Maximum take-off weight is 50,000 pounds. The Warthog is powered by two General Electric TF34-GE-100 turbofan engines producing 9,065 pounds of thrust. Top speed is 439 miles per hour; maximum range is 2,454 miles; service ceiling is 30,500 feet.

The Warthog is one of the "hardest" aircraft flying. The pilot sits in a titanium-armor "bathtub" that can withstand hits from 23mm shells. Control lines are duplicated and stretched through widely separated parts of the aircraft. The heavily armored engines are located high and to the rear for maximum shielding from antiaircraft fire and heat-seeking missiles.

F-117A Stealth
Lockheed F-117A Stealth Fighter—United States

The F-117A Stealth fighter was actually in service for six years before the Air Force even admitted its existence. This super-secret aircraft was born in 1978 at Lockheed's so-called "Skunk Works" in Burbank, California, which has developed so many other advanced aircraft for the Air Force. Configured in the shape of a large, flat delta, or arrowhead, the F-117A was designed to be virtually invisible to radar, and difficult to spot with the naked eye as well.

The F-117A is a single-seat, twin-engine aircraft with a cockpit set low in the front of the fuselage. The engines, buried in the wing roots and deeply recessed to minimize their infrared signature, are set above the fuselage centerline. The skin covering is composed of small, flat surfaces that reflect radar signals in every direction. Almost all of the external surface is coated with radar-absorbent material.

The F-117A Stealth is virtually invisible to radar.

Wobbly Goblin

The aircraft is equipped with fly-by-wire controls, which suggest that it is unstable in flight and needs the constant attention of the flight control computer to keep it flying. It is a highly maneuverable aircraft, but due to its outlandish appearance and the bumpy ride it affords those who fly it, it has come to be known as the "Wobbly Goblin."

The F-117A is powered by two General Electric F404-GE-F1D2 turbofan engines, each delivering 11,000 pounds of thrust. Wingspan is 43 feet, length is 66 feet, height is 13 feet; maximum take-off weight is 52,500 pounds. The top speed of the Stealth is Mach 0.9; maximum range is 1,250 miles and the service ceiling is 52,000 feet.

The Air Force first flew the F-117A in 1981, and from 1981 to 1989 the aircraft was flown only at night to maintain secrecy. The primary mission of the aircraft probably entails low-level precision attacks on high-priority targets with smart bombs or air-to-ground missiles stowed in internal bays. The F-117A received its baptism of fire in December 1989 during the U.S. invasion of Panama, when two Wobbly Goblins flew from Nellis Air Force Base to Panama. The F-117As dropped several 2,000-pound bombs with pinpoint accuracy on the headquarters of two Panamanian infantry divisions at Rio Hato.

GR.Mk1 Jaguar
SEPECAT Jaguar GR.Mk1— Britain

The Jaguar is the result of British/French cooperation.

The Jaguar GR.Mk1 primarily serves as a supersonic attack fighter with the air forces of Britain and France. In 1987 French Jaguars sent to support the government of Chad attacked and drove off Libyan infantry and armored units allied with Chadian anti-government forces.

Joint venture
The Jaguar was the result of a British-French joint development project started in 1965 and completed in 1973. Two companies—British

Aerospace in Britain and Breguet in France—were selected to develop and build the aircraft, forming a joint venture known as SEPECAT.

Between 1973 and 1982, the Royal Air Force received 165 single-seat Jaguars configured for the attack role. The French Air Force acquired 160 single-seat Jaguar variants. All Jaguars were equipped with two Rolls-Royce Adour Mk 102 turbofan engines, each producing 7,306 pounds of thrust. The engines were jointly designed and built by Rolls-Royce of Britain and Turbomecca of France.

The Jaguar has a 29-foot wingspan, and is 55 feet long and 16 feet high. Maximum take-off weight is 34,612 pounds, top speed is Mach 1.1, and maximum range is 1,902 miles. Service ceiling is 45,000 feet.

The Jaguar can carry a mix of cannons and "smart" and gravity bombs. French Jaguars are armed with two DEFA 553 or two Aden 30 millimeter fuselage-mounted guns. A fuselage pylon and four wing pylons can carry up to 10,000 pounds of armament, ranging from nuclear bombs to air-to-ground missiles to rocket pods. The pylons also carry fuel tanks, electronic emission detectors, and jamming pods. Italy also fields a Jaguar-equipped squadron in the Desert Storm offensive.

Tornado
Panavia Tornado—Britain and Italy

In 1969, Britain, West Germany, and Italy formed Panavia, a consortium comprising three

The Tornado is Great Britain's most capable attack plane.

of the largest aircraft manufacturers in Western Europe: British Aerospace, Messerschmitt-Bolkow-Blohm, and Aeritalia. The purpose of this consortium was to design and build a new attack aircraft to NATO criteria.

Panavia subsequently produced the Tornado Interdictor/Strike (IDS) model and the Tornado Air-Defense Variant (ADV). The Tornado made its first flight in August 1974, and initial orders were placed almost immediately by all the countries involved in the project.

Long-distance cruiser

The Tornado is a two-seat aircraft with variable-geometry wings. With the wings swept forward (25 degrees), the aircraft can take off and land at forward airfields not accessible to other fixed wing aircraft; it can also loiter over a specific area or cruise for long distances. With the wings swept back (66 degrees), the Tornado can move quickly to attack advancing enemy aircraft as well as perform close air support missions at high speeds and low altitudes.

The Panavia Tornado IDS has a swept-back wingspan of 28 feet and an unswept wingspan of

46 feet. Length is 55 feet, height is 20 feet, and maximum take-off weight is 60,000 pounds. The Tornado is powered by two Turbo-Union RB-199 Mk 103 turbofan engines producing 16,920 pounds of thrust. Top speed is Mach 2.2 and maximum range is 1,525 miles. Service ceiling is 50,000 feet.

Both IDS and ADV versions are night and all-weather capable. The IDV is armed with two 27 millimeter cannons and up to 19,840 pounds of ordnance (including various missiles, bombs, rocket pods, and electronic countermeasures systems), which are carried on seven fuselage and wing hard points. The Tornado ADV, which is used only by the Royal Air Force, is armed with air-to-air missiles and a 27mm cannon. In addition to the British and Italian air forces, Tornados are flown by the Saudi Arabian air force.

B-52 Stratofortress
Boeing B-52 Stratofortress — United States

Development of the plane that would become the B-52 began in the late 1940s, when the Air Force saw a need for an all-jet bomber that could carry nuclear and conventional bombs more than 4,000 miles. The B-52 made its first flight in 1952 and entered service with the U.S. Air Force's Strategic Air Command (SAC) in 1954.

Prior to the outbreak of hostilities in the Persian Gulf, B-52s had seen extensive combat in the Vietnam War. In 1965, SAC B-52s based in Guam and Thailand began conducting Operation Arc Light carpet bombing raids on Viet Cong

The venerable B-52 has pounded Iraq's ground forces.

strongholds in South Vietnam. In 1972, SAC B-52s began an 11-day series of strategic bombing missions against Hanoi, an action that paved the way for a cease-fire in the war.

"Big Ugly Fat Fellow"

Known as the Big Ugly Fat Fellow (BUFF), the B-52 can carry up to 60,000 pounds of bombs, or a mixture of bombs and air-launched cruise missiles (ALCM) in internal bays and on underwing pylons. A remote-control tail turret is armed with either four .50 caliber machine guns or a 20 millimeter multibarrel cannon for air defense. Advanced electronic systems and terrain-avoidance radar allow for low-level, long-range penetration missions under adverse weather conditions.

The variants presently in U.S. Air Force service are the B-52G and B-52H. The B-52H has a wingspan of 185 feet, and is 161 feet long and 41 feet high. Maximum take-off weight is 488,000 pounds. The B-52H is powered by eight Pratt and Whitney TF33-P-3 turbofan engines, each delivering 13,750 pounds of thrust. The aircraft can attain a top speed of nearly 600 miles per hour; maximum range is 10,145 miles, and service ceiling is 55,000 feet.

Problems with the B-1 strategic bomber (all 91 B-1s in service have been grounded due to problems with the engines) have virtually guaranteed the continued use of the B-52H until the mid-1990s, and probably beyond. In Operation Desert Storm, B-52s were used to conduct round-the-clock carpet bombing attacks against Iraqi troop concentrations and defenses. In addition to high-explosive bombs, the B-52s saturated Iraqi positions with anti-personnel and anti-armor bombs.

F-111/FB-111 Aardvark
General Dynamics F-111/FB-111 Aardvark— United States

About 70 F-111s are active in the Desert Storm campaign.

The F-111 first flew in 1964 under the TFX (tactical fighter, experimental) designation. Entering Air Force service in 1967, it saw action in the Vietnam War, where structural defects and problems with the terrain-following radar contributed to the loss of several aircraft. Withdrawn for modifications, the F-111 returned to combat in 1972, achieving considerable success and earning the nickname "whispering death" from the Viet Cong.

Long-range, deep interdiction

Dubbed Aardvark, the F-111 is now favored by Tactical Air Command (TAC) units for use on long-range, deep-interdiction attacks against targets in enemy territory. The F-111B is used by the Strategic Air Command as a medium bomber.

The F-111 has side-by-side seating for the pilot and weapons system operator, and can fly at Mach 2 speeds. The FB-111 can carry a 16-ton nuclear or conventional bomb load, or 13 tons of bombs and four AGM-69 Short-range Attack Missiles carried on swiveling pylons affixed beneath the variable-geometry wings. A Pave Track laser designator system enables pin-point bombing accuracy. The F-111's wings can be changed in flight from a straight to a swept-back delta configuration.

The F-111F has a swept-back wingspan of 32 feet and an unswept wingspan of 63 feet. Length is 74 feet, height is 17 feet, and maximum take-off weight is 100,000 pounds. Two Pratt and Whitney JF3-P-100 turbofan engines produce 25,100 pounds of thrust. Maximum range is 3,378 miles, and the service ceiling is 60,000 feet.

On April 15, 1986, 18 F-111s supported by U.S. Air Force refueling planes conducted punitive strikes against Libya in reprisal for Libyan sponsorship of terrorist acts. In the opening hours of Operation Desert Storm, F-111s were once again used with great effectiveness to conduct pinpoint bombing missions against Iraqi command and control centers.

E-3 Sentry
Boeing E-3 Sentry (AWACS)— United States

Electronic warfare is directed by the E-3.

The E-3 Sentry is the most sophisticated airborne command post ever devised. The airframe chosen for the job was the Boeing Model 707, which was equipped with state-of-the-art electronics inside and topped with a 30-foot rotating radome. The aircraft are designated AWACS; the acronym stands for Airborne Warning and Control System.

The first of two dozen E-3A Sentrys were delivered in 1977, and all 24 went into service on January 1, 1979. Although flown by the Air Force Tactical Air Command, they first saw duty with the joint U.S./Canadian North American Air Defense Command (NORAD).

New and improved

An improvement program begun in 1984 has seen the A model superseded by the E-3B and the E-3C. The improvements have included more situation display consoles (SDC), a better radar jamming system, and an upgraded Joint Tactical Information Distribution System (JTIDS) and Tactical Digital Information Link (TADIL).

The Boeing E-3 Sentry is 153 feet long, 42 feet high, and has a wingspan of 146 feet and a maximum take-off weight of 325,000 pounds. Four Pratt and Whitney TF33-PW-100/100A turbofan engines each deliver 21,000 pounds of thrust. Top speed is 530 miles per hour; maximum range is 7,475 miles; service ceiling is 29,000 feet.

As the world discovered when a U.S. Navy warship shot down an Iranian civilian passenger airliner over the Persian Gulf in 1988, battlefield electronics are only as good as the people who operate them. Similarly, the decisions these people make in the heat of battle are only as good as the information they receive. This makes IFF (Identification, Friend or Foe) recognition of aircraft a vital part of the AWACS task. Upon detecting enemy aircraft, the E-3s can vector friendly fighters to the optimal attack position.

The E-3 is also used to guide bombers to their targets. In Operation Desert Storm, the AWACS planes formed an interlocking, yet noninterfering, network of command posts able to manage the hundreds of warplanes that might be conducting attack sorties and combat air patrols at any given moment.

F-4G Wild Weasel
McDonnell Douglas F-4G Wild Weasel— United States

Wild Weasels disable enemy radar positions.

Like a wonderful old fire horse, the McDonnell Douglas F-4G Phantom is back in action, this time in the absolutely vital role of "Wild Weasel," suppressing Iraqi radars and missile sites.

Indomitable warhorse
The F-4 is without question the single most important fighter to emerge in the free world in

the last two decades. Originally submitted by McDonnell as a speculative bid, the F-4 became the mainstay of three services—the Air Force, the Navy, and the Marines. In addition to use by 11 foreign countries, it is still in front-line American service 32 years after its first flight. (To put this in perspective, similar longevity for the World War I Spad would have permitted it to fly in the Korean War.)

The first Wild Weasels came into being to suppress the Soviet-built SA-2 SAMs and "Fan Song" radars that the North Vietnamese were using in 1965. North American F-100 Sabres were used first, but as the program developed, both Republic F-105 and McDonnell Douglas F-4 aircraft were successfully pressed into service.

The F-4G Wild Weasel seeks out radar emitters and then launches AGM-88 HARM or AGM-45A Shrike missiles. The High-speed Antiradiation Missile (HARM) was the key to the incredible success in Iraq of the F-4G Weasel crews. The HARM has an excellent stand-off capability combined with fantastic accuracy and devastating power. HARMs can work even if they are not fired, for enemy radars will often just shut down rather than run the risk of destruction. When this happens, the attacking "force package" can get in almost undetected.

The F-4G Wild Weasel has a wingspan of 39 feet, and is 63 feet long and 16 feet high. Maximum take-off weight is 60,630 pounds; maximum range is 2,300 miles. The service ceiling is 59,000 feet. The Wild Weasel is powered by two General Electric J79-15 turbojets, each delivering 17,900 pounds of thrust, and can attain a top speed of 1,464 miles per hour.

The F-4G's are aging, and getting adequate spare parts is one of the most difficult tasks confronting the Air Force.

AH-64A Apache
McDonnell Douglas AH-64A Apache—United States

The Apache is every bit as lethal as it looks.

The AH-64A Apache is specifically designed for the attack role. The first production model was rolled out on September 30, 1983, and the first delivery to the Army was made on January 26 of the following year.

The Apache is armed with a McDonnell Douglas M230 30 millimeter multibarrel cannon and up to 16 laser-guided Hellfire missiles. The Hellfire has a range of more than 3.7 miles and can penetrate the armor of any known main battle tank. The Apache may also be armed with 2.75-inch folding-fin aerial rockets. All rockets are carried on two stub wings that provide additional lift and may serve as attaching points for external fuel tanks.

Hard to kill

The Apache was designed to be crashworthy. Armor made of boron carbide bonded to Kevlar protects the Apache crew and the helicopter's vital systems. Blast shields, which protect against 23mm rounds or smaller high-explosive incendiary ammunition, separate the pilot and copilot/weapons system operator; thus, both crew members cannot be incapacitated by a single round. Armored seats and airframe armor can withstand .50 caliber rounds.

The Apache's main rotor has four blades made of stainless steel spars and fiberglass tubes. They can cut through tree branches up to two inches in diameter or withstand 23mm high-explosive shell strikes. Fuel cells, located forward and aft of the ammunition bay, are self-sealing and can absorb the impact of 23mm rounds.

The AH-64A Apache has a main rotor diameter of 48 feet and a tail rotor diameter of nine feet. Power is supplied by two General Electric T700-701 turboshaft engines providing 1,694 horsepower each. The aircraft is 48 feet long, 12 feet high, and can weigh 21,000 pounds maximum at take-off. Top speed is 184 miles per hour, range is 300 miles, and service ceiling is 21,000 feet.

AH-1S HueyCobra
AH-1S HueyCobra
(Bell Model 209)—
United States

In 1965, Bell Helicopter introduced a specific Huey variant to serve as an armed escort helicopter for transport and medevac choppers. The initial model designation of the HueyCobra was AH-1G. Distinguishing features included a new, thin-profile fuselage and stub wings designed to ease the load on the main rotor and serve as attaching points for additional weapons. The narrow fuselage dictated a tandem cockpit seating arrangement, with the pilot placed behind and above the copilot.

The HueyCobra targets Iraqi tanks.

Fly 'n' fire

A turret was mounted under the nose of the fuselage to carry miniguns, rapid-firing cannons, or grenade launchers. The weapons are controlled by the copilot, who is also designated the weapons operator. When the copilot/weapons operator releases the weapon controls, the turret resumes a locked fore and aft position and the pilot can fire the turret guns while flying the helicopter. Aiming in this instance is done by turning the helicopter toward the target. The copilot/weapons operator can also fly the helicopter.

The first HueyCobra model to be armed with the BGM-71 TOW antitank missile was the AH-1Q, which was intended as an interim solution until the modernized HueyCobra, the AH-1S, could be developed. The first AH-1S entered Army service in March 1977. Subsequent AH-1S variants were equipped with a universal turret mounting either a 20 millimeter or 30mm gun.

The AH-1S HueyCobra's main rotor is 44 feet in diameter, and the tail rotor is 9 feet in diameter. The AH-1S is powered by a Lycoming T53-L-703 1,800-horsepower turboshaft engine. The aircraft is 45 feet long, 13 feet high, and has a maximum take-off weight of 10,000 pounds. Top speed is 141 miles per hour, and the maximum range is 315 miles. Service ceiling is 12,200 feet.

Harpoon
Harpoon Antiship Missile— United States

The Harpoon, which is one of world's deadliest antiship missiles, began its life in 1968 as an air-to-surface missile and quickly showed an improbable flexibility. Today, the Harpoon is a short- to medium-range, all-weather missile that can be launched from aircraft, and from ships and submarines as well.

Sea-skimming flight
The Harpoon is 15 feet long, a little over one foot in diameter, and weighs 1,498 pounds.

The Harpoon missile is deadly and versatile.

Armed with a 500-pound high-explosive fragmentation warhead, the missile skims over the waves at a speed of Mach .75 to a range of more than 69 miles. In a standard launch the Harpoon, which is controlled by an inertial autopilot and radar altimeter, traces a ballistic path during the boost phase, then descends to a few feet above the water. During the final stages of flight, the Harpoon's active radar switches on and guides the missile the rest of the way to its target.

In the past, the Harpoon performed a "terminal maneuver," which meant that it would suddenly fly upward, or "pop up," then dive on the target. This maneuver has been discontinued because it made the Harpoon vulnerable to the increasingly effective anti-missile defense systems found on modern warships.

A variant of the Harpoon is the Standoff Land Attack Missile (SLAM), which entered Navy service in 1989. SLAM, which is mounted on A-6E Intruders and F/A-18 Hornets for use against land targets, is designed to hit its target with a minimum of collateral damage to nearby populated areas and structures. Immediately following launch, SLAM is guided by signals received from navigation satellites. When SLAM comes within visual range of its target, an infrared TV camera mounted in the nose sends pictures back to the airborne weapons operator, who uses the images to accurately guide the missile to the point of impact.

Sidewinder and Maverick
Sidewinder and Maverick Missiles — United States

While some notable new weapons have been introduced into service in the war with Iraq, the U.S. military and many of its allies continue to rely on a number of missiles of demonstrated reliability and performance. Two of these are the heat-seeking Sidewinder and the optically guided Maverick.

Old but effective

In terms of years of operation, the AIM-9 Sidewinder air-to-air missile may be considered an elderly weapon. However, almost continuous upgrading has kept it at the forefront of guided missiles used around the world. A heat-seeker, the Sidewinder is now far more capable of maneuver than it was during its Vietnam days.

A Maverick missile is inspected before a flight test.

Unlike many of its contemporaries, the Sidewinder is considered by the Air Force to still have room for further development. The Air Force will probably be using the missile well into the next century. The Sidewinder is 10 feet long, weighs 191 pounds at launch, and carries a 21-pound warhead. Maximum range is 10 miles.

Another old standby is the AGM-65 Maverick air-to-ground missile, which has an automatic homing capability that enables the pilot to acquire a target, fire the round, and have the Maverick automatically track into the target. The missile is a little over 8 feet long, weighs 462 pounds at launch, and carries an 83-pound warhead. Maximum range is 14 miles.

The Maverick has gained worldwide acceptance, and is used by 18 Allied nations. The latest U.S. versions have a refinement badly needed in Iraq: the ability to determine by infrared radiation detection whether its target is a "live" tank or just a hulk.

Phoenix
Phoenix Missile System — United States

The Phoenix's range is more than 120 miles.

The six carrier battle groups operating in waters of the Gulf theater of war carry the most sophisticated fighter in history and one whose longevity may be extended well into the 21st century: The Grumman F-14 Tomcat. Continuously improved since its introduction, the F-14 has assumed a new lease on life as a candidate to replace the canceled A-12 stealth attack plane.

The heart of the Tomcat's unmatched prowess is the combination of its Phoenix missile system and a powerful AWG-9 radar system. A similar combination—of radar and Sidewinder and Sparrow missiles—had proved itself in 1981, and again in 1989, when Libyan planes made the mistake of tangling with American F-14s in the Mediterranean. In the first instance, a pair of Soviet-built Sukhoi 22 attack jets were splashed by Sidewinders; in the second, a pair of more modern, Soviet-built MiG-23 fighters that had been launched at the aircraft carrier USS *John F. Kennedy* were downed by Sidewinder and Sparrow missiles.

Long-range winner

As impressive as these kills were, the Phoenix air-to-air missile system possesses capabilities far in excess of that of either Sidewinder or Sparrow. The AWG-9 radar can detect and track up to 24 targets simultaneously, from as low as 50 feet above the surface to above 80,000 feet. The Phoenix's range—better than 120 miles—is unmatched by any other air-launched missile.

The first part of the missile's flight is inertially guided. Phoenix then acquires the target on its own homing radar and, from that point on, homes in with unerring accuracy. The Phoenix is 13 feet long, weighs 985 pounds at launch, and carries a 132-pound warhead.

At more than a million dollars apiece, the Phoenix missiles seem extremely expensive, until you realize that the performance they offer is the best protection for a multi-billion-dollar aircraft carrier, as well as the priceless lives of the men who serve on it.

Hellfire Missile
Laser Hellfire Missile— United States

Many missiles have far more of a mixed lineage than do aircraft. It used to be that weapon systems were crafted by an individual manufacturer,

The Hellfire missile is laser-guided.

and bore a distinctive stamp. Today a typical missile may be built by Boeing, have a Lockheed rocket powerplant, and guidance by General Precision/Kearfott.

The Hellfire AGM-114A missile has a simpler pedigree, descended as it is from the Rockwell International Hornet (ZAGM-64A), a precision air-launched missile designed to test the feasibility of television and electro-optical guidance systems. The Hornet's technology was used by a number of other missiles before leading to the Hellfire anti-armor weapon system.

Laser homing

The Hellfire has a semi-active laser homing device, which incorporates a seeker head that searches for the signal, then follows the reflected laser energy to the target. Because the laser signal comes from another source, the launcher—helicopter or aircraft—can "fire and forget." In its test program, the Hellfire was also matched with a number of other homers, including both infrared and television.

The Rockwell laser homing device used on the Hellfire is also used on other smart bombs and missiles, including the GBU-15 and the updated Mavericks.

The Hellfire is five feet 10 inches long and weighs 98 pounds at launch; its warhead weighs 20 pounds. Maximum range depends upon the altitude from which the Hellfire is launched; generally, the range is several miles.

One important characteristic of the Hellfire is its adaptability to a wide variety of weapons platforms, ranging from ground-launch vehicles to helicopters to the A-10A Thunderbolt II. The laser designators can be immensely sophisticated, or as simple as a foot soldier using a hand-held laser-designating device.

HARM Missile
AGA-88 HARM Missile— United States

One of the most pleasant surprises that greeted United Nations commanders in the Gulf War was both the success of the McDonnell Douglas F-4G Wild Weasels, and their low attrition rate in one of the toughest jobs of the war: suppression of Iraqi radar and missile sites. The HARM (High-speed Anti-Radiation Missile) has helped the F-4G to perform that job.

Fantastic accuracy distinguishes the HARM missile.

Tough task

During the Vietnam War, the debut of a formidable North Vietnamese system of radars and surface-to-air missile (SAM) batteries posed such a devastating threat to U.S. airpower that immediate steps were taken to develop a defense suppression capability. The Wild Weasel's task was daunting from the start because the American pilots were given the task of invading enemy airspace, making themselves a target for the North Vietnamese SAMs. When the North Vietnamese radars picked them up, the Wild Weasels would attack in a headlong race to see if they would knock out the radars before the SAMs—or the murderous antiaircraft installations which surrounded them—got them.

By 1965 most Air Force F-4 and F-105 aircraft and all Navy attack planes were armed with the AGM-65 Shrike missile, which has been continually improved over the years and remains a standard weapon.

The AGM-88A HARM, a much more sophisticated air-to-ground missile, was developed in the immediate post-Vietnam era.

In the F-4G, the HARM is tied into the highly effective APR-38 electronic warfare system, which acts as a central processor for first detecting, then analyzing and locating enemy radar emitters. The HARM is a big missile—some 13 feet 9 inches in length, and weighing 807 pounds at launch; its warhead weighs 145 pounds. The HARM has a maximum range of 16 miles. Accuracy has proved to be fantastically good, for even when the enemy radar transmitter shuts down the HARM "remembers" its location and proceeds to destroy it.

Land Weaponry

An M-60 MBT describes a course across desert terrain.

With regard to America's involvement in wars past, the advent of hostilities usually found the U.S. Army woefully lacking in manpower, training, and equipment for the task at hand. Operation Desert Storm represents a welcome departure from this tradition of unpreparedness. Indeed, the ground force America deployed for war against Iraq was in many respects the finest army this nation has ever committed to the field of modern-day battle. Although largely untested in actual combat (excepting the veterans of Vietnam and the campaigns in Grenada and Panama), the various elements of this all-volunteer army have been maintained at the peak of readiness, training, and advanced technology.

At the outbreak of Operation Desert Storm, the United States Army had in place in the

Saudi Arabian desert some 245,000 troops, 1,200 main battle tanks, 2,200 armored personnel carriers, and 1,700 helicopters. The Army force was joined by a Marine component comprising 75,000 troops and 200 tanks. The combined Army/Marine force was further augmented by 265,000 Allied troops, mostly from Britain, France, Saudi Arabia, and Egypt. Arrayed against them were 545,000 Iraqi front-line troops, nearly 500,000 reservists, 4,200 tanks, and 2,800 armored personnel carriers.

M-1 and M-1A1 Abrams
M-1 and M-1A1 Abrams Main Battle Tank— United States

The first M-1 tanks were delivered to the U.S. Army on February 28, 1980. The new tank was named for the late General Creighton W. Abrams, former Army Chief of Staff and commander of the 37th Armored Battalion.

Protection against chemical agents

The M-1 mounts an M68E1 105 millimeter main gun. Two 7.62mm NATO M240 machine guns are also mounted, one coaxially with the main gun, and one on top of the turret at the loader's station. A .50 caliber Browning M2 HB machine gun is mounted at the commander's station for anti-aircraft defense. The M-1A1, first delivered in

The M-1 is the U.S. Army's most advanced tank.

August 1985, mounts an M256 smoothbore Rheinmetall main gun developed in West Germany. M-1A1 upgrades also involved enhanced armor protection and a new nuclear-biological-chemical warfare protection system.

The Abrams hull and turret are built of a material similar to the ceramic-and-steel-plate Chobham armor developed in Britain. The driver is seated in a reclining position in the front of the hull; the commander and gunner are in the turret on the right, and the loader is on the left. Armor plate separates the crew compartment from the fuel tanks and ammunition storage area.

Despite its 63-ton weight, the M-1A1 can attain a top speed of 45 miles per hour. The tank is 26 feet long, 12 feet wide, and eight feet high. Range is limited to 290 miles.

In March 1988 a program to develop and mount depleted uranium armor plate on the M-1A1 was begun. A non-radioactive substance, depleted uranium has a density at least two-and-a-half times greater than steel. The depleted uranium armor will raise the total weight of the Abrams tank to 65 tons, but offers vastly improved protection in the bargain.

Immediately following President Bush's decision to commit U.S. forces to Saudi Arabia, American armored units began the difficult process of relocating to the threatened area. The M-1A1's arrival was much welcomed by Allied forces, as it is capable of defeating any tank in the Iraqi inventory.

M-60
M-60 Main Battle Tank— United States

The M-60's main gun fires 6-8 rounds per minute.

The M-60 Main Battle Tank (MBT) entered service in 1960 as a replacement for its predecessor, the M-48 Patton Medium Tank. More than 15,000 M-60s of various configurations were built before production ceased in August 1987. The latest variant is the M-60A3.

The M-60 hull is built of cast-and-welded sections and divided into three compartments: driving, fighting, and engine/transmission. The turret mounts an L7A1 105 millimeter M68 main gun. Of British design but built in the United States, the main gun is rifled and can fire between six and eight rounds per minute. The tank carries 63 rounds of 105mm ammunition. The M-60 also mounts two machine guns: a .50 caliber M85 antiaircraft gun in the commander's cupola, and a 7.62mm NATO M73 gun mounted coaxially in the turret.

Laser range finder

A nuclear-biological-chemical warfare protection system was added in the M-60A3 configuration, as well as night vision equipment. It also has an AN/VVG-2 laser range finder connected to an improved fire control system that uses an M21 solid state computer. The new system allows either the gunner or the tank commander to fire the main gun.

The M-60A3 is 23 feet long, 11 feet high, and 12 feet wide. It weighs in at 58 tons and can attain a top speed of 30 mph. Range is approximately 300 miles.

The M-60A3 has a track system with replaceable pads. An automatic Halon fire extinguisher system, a smoke-screen system and the M219 smoke grenade launcher have also been installed. A deep-water fording kit allows an M-60A3 fitted with a snorkel to traverse water up to 13 feet deep. Most of the General Dynamics-built M-60A3s have been updated with reactive armor, essential against Saddam Hussein's forces.

Challenger
Challenger Main Battle Tank—Britain

The Challenger is one of the world's best tanks.

The Challenger Main Battle Tank (MBT) became operational in 1983. Like its predecessor, the Chieftain, the Challenger is an accommodation of firepower, armor protection, and speed and agility. The turret and hull are protected by Chobham armor and steel plate armor. Chobham armor is a compound made up of plastic, ceramic, and steel plates, and is designed to absorb and deflect kinetic rounds and protect against shaped-charge gas plasma jets.

The Challenger's main armament is the 120 millimeter L11A5 rifled gun. The tank is also armed with two 7.62mm NATO machine guns, one mounted coaxially with the main gun, the other mounted near the commander's cupola for antiaircraft defense.

The Challenger has a gunnery and sighting system that incorporates a laser range finder and a thermal imaging system for use at night, in smoke, or in fog. A gun sighting system known as TOGS—Thermal Observation and Gunnery System—is now being installed in Challengers.

The Challenger is 28 feet long, eight feet high, and 12 feet wide. It weighs 68 tons, and can attain a top speed of 35 miles per hour. Maximum range is 250 miles.

Slow but formidable

The Challenger's fire control system does not seem to be as accurate or as fast as that of the M-1 Abrams. Evidently, the TOGS sight cannot scan independently of the turret's own movement. This reduces the commander's ability to search for new targets while the gunner fires on the current target. The Challenger is somewhat slower than the M-1 Abrams and the Soviet T-72. Nevertheless, the Challenger is in most respects a formidable tank, inasmuch as it is more heavily armed and armored than its counterparts. And it is certain that British soldiers, in writing yet another chapter in their long history of desert warfare, will have good cause to be proud of the Challenger's performance.

T-72
T-72 Main Battle Tank—Iraq

Production of the T-72 Main Battle Tank is thought to have started in 1972. The T-72 is well protected by 11-inch armor on the turret face and 8.8 inches of spaced, laminate armor on the hull nose, which is angled to provide the equivalent of 21.5 inches of armor.

The capable T-72 is heavily armed and armored.

The tank mounts a 125 millimeter smoothbore Model 2A465 main gun, which is fed from an automatic carousel loader mounted on the hull floor. The main gun is stabilized, allowing the T-72 to shoot on the move. A 7.62mm machine gun is mounted in the turret coaxially with the main gun and can be fired automatically. A 12.7mm DShKM machine gun is mounted ahead of the hatch on the commander's cupola.

Radiation protection

The T-72 mounts an infrared searchlight on the right side of the main gun. It also carries a snorkel clipped to the left side of the turret, and has full nuclear-biological-chemical protection. The interior of the tank is also lined with a lead-impregnated material for protection against radiation and neutron pulses.

Israeli tanks operating in Lebanon in 1982 destroyed a large number of Syrian-manned T-72s. Since then, the Soviets have enhanced the tank's survivability with the installation of appliqué armor, fender skirts, and reaction armor boxes.

The T-72 is 23 feet long, eight feet high, and 12 feet wide. It weighs 45.2 tons, which is considerably less than the M-1 Abrams and the British Challenger. The tank can attain a top speed of 37 miles per hour, and has a range of 300 miles.

To date, an estimated 17,000 T-72 tanks have been built. In addition to Iraq, the T-72 has been distributed to 14 nations in Eastern Europe, the Middle East, and Africa. Iraq's initial deployment of its 500-odd T-72 tanks was highly conservative, digging them in the familiar triangular "forts" that were developed in the war with Iran.

T-62
T-62 Main Battle Tank—Iraq

The T-62 Main Battle Tank (MBT) entered production in 1962, and an estimated 20,000 units were built during the next eight years. The T-62's main gun is the 115 millimeter U-5TS smoothbore. One 7.62mm PKT machine gun is mounted coaxially, and a 12.7mm DShKM machine gun is mounted on the turret for antiaircraft defense.

The T-62's turret is cast in one piece and has 9.5-inch thick armor on its forward face. The T-62 and T-62A have been updated with a laser range finder, a solid-state ballistic computer, new infrared driving lights and searchlights, and an image intensifier for night combat. Appliqué and reaction armor have also been installed on some T-62s.

The T-62 has a nuclear radiation protection system that automatically seals the tank when a

The T-62 has the low profile typical of Soviet MBTs.

preset level of radiation is encountered. A blower and filtration system removes radiation-contaminated dust and other particles. There is no biological or chemical protection system, and the crew must wear contamination suits.

The T-62 is 22 feet long, eight feet high, and 11 feet wide. It weighs 44 tons, and can attain a top speed of 31 miles per hour. Maximum range is 280 miles.

More tanks than Hitler

The T-62 has several significant flaws. Its main gun cannot be aimed low enough to deal with attacking infantry, and its rate of fire is slowed by a complicated fire control system. Moreover, the main gun elevates after recoil, and the turret cannot be traversed during the loading sequence.

Consequently, the T-62 was consistently defeated by Israeli tanks during the 1973 Yom Kippur War and the 1982 invasion of Lebanon. Despite its drawbacks, however, it is used by some 23 countries. Prior to the Desert Storm offensive, Iraq had more than 1,000 T-62As in its inventory—far more than the number of heavy tanks that Hitler's armies used in their 1940 blitzkrieg against Western Europe.

T-55
T-54/T-55 Main Battle Tank— Iraq

Though widely used by Iraq, the T-55 is obsolete.

Design work on the T-54/T-55 series of Main Battle Tanks began shortly after World War II, with the first T-54 prototype being produced in 1946. The T-54 mounted a 100 millimeter Model 1944 main gun, and had a turret that was cast in one piece with the top welded on. The T-54 mounted two 7.62mm machine guns, one in the hull and the other coaxially in the turret. A 12.7mm DShKM machine gun was mounted on the turret at the loader's cupola for antiaircraft defense.

The T-55 model entered service in 1959 or 1960. Essentially an improved T-54, it is distinguished by a more powerful engine, a rotating turret floor, the elimination of the loader's cupola, and an improved transmission. The 12.7mm antiaircraft machine gun and the 7.62mm machine gun mounted in the bow plate were removed in the T-55A version to allow more room for 100mm ammunition. The T-55A was given an antiradiation lining, although no version of the T-54 or T-55 has true nuclear-biological-chemical warfare protection for its crew.

The T-55 is 21 feet long, eight feet high, and 11 feet wide. It weighs nearly 40 tons, and can attain a top speed of 31 miles per hour. Maximum range is 373 miles.

Past its prime

An estimated 57,000 T-54 and T-55 tanks have been built. The T-55 is still in wide use with former Warsaw Pact forces, and with Iraq as well. It is a tank that is clearly past its prime. On January 29-30, 1991, Iraqi armored and infantry probes involving scores of T-55s were launched against Saudi and U.S. Marine positions in Saudi Arabia; the coalition forces, using TOW antitank rockets and assisted by attack helicopters and A-6E and A-10 attack planes, repulsed the attack, destroying an estimated 24 enemy tanks in the process.

M2/M3 Bradley
M2/M3 Bradley Infantry and Cavalry Fighting Vehicles—United States

The M2 Bradley quickly brings troops to battle.

Selected for use in 1976, the M2/M3 Bradley fighting vehicle was designed specifically to carry infantry troops into battle in support of tanks, and to help consolidate gains made by armor.

The Bradley weighs 25 tons and is capable of traveling 41 miles per hour on a hard surface. With its tracks providing propulsion through water, the Bradley can swim at a speed of 4.2 miles per hour. The vehicle's cruising range is 300 miles. It can pivot on its own axis, climb 60-degree slopes and 36-inch walls, and cross trenches 100 inches wide. The Bradley is 21 feet long, ten feet high, and 11 feet wide.

Accuracy on rough terrain

The M2 Infantry Fighting Vehicle (IFV) and the M3 Cavalry Fighting Vehicle (CFV) are both armed with a turret-mounted M242 25 millimeter chain gun. The M242 can be fired accurately while the vehicle is moving at speed over rough terrain. An M240C 7.62 millimeter coaxial machine gun is mounted to the right of the main gun. Additional armament includes seven TOW missiles fired from a launcher mounted on the left side of the turret. The TOWs are capable of defeating Soviet main battle tanks at an extreme range of 3,000 yards.

The M2 IFV carries a nine-man infantry squad, as well as six ball-mounted M231 Colt 5.56mm port-firing automatic weapons. The infantry troops can fight from inside the Bradley then quickly exit to fight outside the vehicle. The M3 CFV has a crew of five, carries more 25mm ammunition than the IFV, and has 10 additional TOWs. In open terrain such as that encountered in the Desert Storm offensive, the Bradley can significantly reduce casualties even as it helps to enhance the offensive capability of an attacking armored force.

A current version, the M113A3, is provided with external fuel tanks and spall-suppressant, bolt-on interior armor to increase crew survivability. An uprated powertrain that, even with the added armor, increases the vehicle's cross country speed to 22 miles per hour is available. The M113A3 is armed with a .50 caliber M2 machine gun with 2000 rounds. Basic hull armor is 5083 aluminum. Bottom surfaces have anti-mine appliqués. The M113A3 is not fast enough to keep pace with the M-1 Abrams tank, so is retained only in mechanized units having the M-60 main battle tank.

LAV-25
Marine Corps Light Assault Vehicle 25—United States

The versatile LAV-25 has a top speed of 63 mph.

The U.S. Marine Corps' Light Assault Vehicle 25 (LAV-25) is an eight-wheeled armored fighting vehicle (AFV) and personnel carrier. Designed by MOWAG of Kreuzlingen, Switzerland, the LAV-25 is armed with a stabilized Hughes M242 Bushmaster 25mm chain gun and a coaxial M240C 7.62 machine gun mounted in a power-driven, two-man turret. The LAV-25 can also mount an Mk19 40mm grenade launcher, M2 .50-inch machine gun, or M60 7.62 machine gun on a turret-pintle mount. The 25mm Bushmaster fires Armor Piercing Discarding Sabot (APDS) and

High-Explosive Incendiary Tracer (HEI-T) ammunition, defeating all Soviet or Warsaw Pact light-armored vehicles and armored personnel carriers at 8,202 feet.

The LAV-25 is 21 feet long, eight feet high, and seven feet wide. The vehicle weighs just under 14 tons, and can attain a top speed of 63 miles per hour on smooth surfaces. Maximum range is 485 miles.

Many versions, many roles

Six versions of the LAV-25 are currently in service: the LAV-25 with 25mm chain-gun; LAV logistics carrier; LAV mortar vehicle armed with the 81mm mortar; LAV anti-tank vehicle carrying a twin TOW missile launcher; LAV command and control vehicle; and the LAV maintenance/recovery vehicle. Under consideration is the LAV-90 variant, which mounts a Belgian MECAR Kenerga 90mm high-velocity, low recoil gun.

The LAV-25 carries a three-man crew (commander, driver, and gunner), with room for six combat-ready marines in the cargo compartment. Marines sit three to a side, facing outboard, and fire their weapons through ports. The vehicle is air transportable, carried inside the Lockheed C-130 Hercules, C-141 Starlifter, and the C-5 Galaxy. It can also be carried in a sling beneath the Boeing CH-53E Super Sea Stallion helicopter; the copter can ferry the LAV-25 from landing-assault ships directly to the beach.

M998 (HMMWV)
M998 High Mobility, Multi-purpose Wheeled Vehicle (HMMWV)—United States

The "Hummer" is a marked improvement over the Jeep.

The HMMWV is a 1¾-ton, four-wheel drive, multi-faceted utility vehicle designed to fill a variety of military roles for modern ground forces. Popularly known as the HummVee, or Hummer, it was adopted by the U.S. armed forces in 1982 to replace the aging series of Jeep vehicles. It can also supplant the M274 half-ton MULE, the 1¼-ton M880 pickup truck, and the M792 1¼-ton ambulance in their respective roles. A low silhouette profile and high maneuvering rate allow the Hummer to offer much greater flexibility in terms of battlefield movement than the vehicles it replaces. Top speed is 65 mph; range is 300 miles.

A multifunctional vehicle

At least 60,000 Hummers have been delivered to the U.S. Army, Air Force, and Marines Corps. The Hummer family of vehicles consists of up to 18 different variations. Mounting TOW antitank missile systems, the Hummer can function in a tank-busting "shoot and scoot" role. It can also be armed with 7.62 millimeter and .50 caliber machine guns, and the Mk 19 grenade launcher system. Additionally, the Hummer can provide battlefield assistance as a staff car, supply wagon, troop carrier, communications center, command post, medical evacuation vehicle, and weapons carrier.

For ease of repair and maintenance, all Hummers are built with the same chassis, engine, and transmission. Although still in the early stages of its service career, the Hummer has already proved itself a tough combat vehicle.

M198 Howitzer
M198 155mm Towed Howitzer—United States

First production models of the M198 Howitzer were delivered to the U.S. Army and Marine Corps in 1978. It is expected that the M198 will be America's premier towed field artillery piece for many years to come.

The M198 can be lifted by the CH-47 and CH-53E helicopters, prime movers respectively of the Army and Marine Corps. The M939 five-ton

The M198 Howitzer has tremendous range.

truck is the weapon's other prime mover. The M198 and its recoil mechanism are mounted on a split-trail carriage. The carriage wheels are mounted on a two-position suspension system so that the wheels can be lifted up and out of contact with the ground by a hand-operated hydraulic pump. In the firing position, the M198 sits solidly on its firing platform without having to be anchored, and its long trails are opened into a wide "V". The cannon itself is transported either with the barrel forward or rotated to rest aft along the trails.

Less than five minutes to fire

The M198's gun tube is fitted with a screw-on, double-baffle muzzle brake. The barrel can be elevated by hand to an angle of 71 degrees for firing at close range, and it can be depressed to five degrees below centerline for transporting or for point-blank firing. The gun fires a full range of U.S. separate-loading 155 millimeter ammunition, and a trained crew of 11 needs less than five minutes to tow the M198 into position and ready it for firing.

The M198 has a 20-foot barrel, and is 41 feet long overall. It can fire at a sustained rate of two rounds per minute, and a maximum rate of four rounds per minute. Conventional ammunition range is 24,059 yards.

If there was one area where the Iraqi army possessed clear superiority at the outbreak of the conflict, it was in artillery. Yet U.S. artillery batteries, while not nearly so numerous, could nevertheless consider themselves well-armed with the excellent M198.

M109 Howitzer
M109 155mm Self-propelled Howitzer—United States

The M109 Self-propelled 155 millimeter Howitzer is the standard direct support artillery weapon in U.S. armored and mechanized infantry units. It carries a crew of six: commander, gunner, driver, and three ammunition handlers. The driver sits in the left front portion of the hull, with the engine to his right. Command and gunnery stations are located in the turret. The hull and turret are built of welded aluminum. The armor, also aluminum, is reinforced with Kevlar antispalling liners. The M109A2/3 turret has a

The M109 Howitzer carries a crew of six.

full-width bustle that carries 22 rounds of 155 millimeter ammunition.

The M109A2/3 weighs nearly 28 tons, can maintain a road speed of 33 miles per hour, and ford streams as deep as six feet at four miles per hour. The main armament is the 16.66-foot M185 155mm cannon, which fires a conventional high-explosive round to a range of 19,794 yards. When firing a rocket-assisted projectile, the M109A2/3 can achieve ranges up to 26,246 yards. The gun can fire one round per minute or, for short periods, three rounds per minute. The gun tube, which is 17 feet long, can be elevated to 75 degrees, depressed five degrees below centerline, and traversed 360 degrees. All gun controls are hydraulic and have manual backup.

A range of ammunition

The M109A2/3 can fire a complete range of U.S. 155mm ammunition, including high-explosive, smoke, illumination, tactical nuclear, chemical, and rocket-assisted high explosive rounds. Secondary armament is a .50 caliber M2 heavy-barrel machine gun mounted on the turret near the commander's station.

All told, the M109 is a highly mobile weapon perfectly suited to providing artillery support in the fast-changing conditions of armored warfare in the desert.

Multiple Launch Rocket System
Multiple Launch Rocket System (MLRS)— United States

The Multiple Launch Rocket System (MLRS), developed by LTV for the U.S. Army and Marine Corps, is designed for medium-interdiction fire missions. It is capable of dealing devastating blows to a fast-moving enemy within the Forward Edge of the Battle Area (FEBA). As such, it is ideal for use against the kind of entrenched, tri-angular fortresses the Iraqis constructed to withstand Operation Desert Storm. The MLRS consists of a launcher, free rockets, a computerized aim and control complex, and a tracked vehicle. The system is capable of multiple launchings of up to 12 rockets in one minute. Maximum range of the rockets is 18 miles.

Bradley provides transport

The system's tracked Armored Vehicle Mounted Rocket Launcher (AVMRL) uses the same chassis

The MLRS packs a devastating punch.

as the M2 Bradley Infantry Fighting Vehicle. The AVMRL has a range of 300 miles, a top speed of 40 miles per hour, and considerable off-the-road capability. The Launcher Loader Module (LLM) is bolted to the vehicle bed and can be raised to 60 degrees and traversed in a complete circle. It carries 12 rockets. Two boom-mounted electrical cable hoists are used by crew members to reload the two rocket pods.

The MLRS rocket is a tube-launched, free-flight weapon weighing approximately 667 pounds, and is 13 feet long. Inside the warhead are polyurethane foam containers holding 644 individual M77 anti-personnel/anti-materiel submunitions, which are effective against troops and light armor. When the MLRS rocket reaches the target area, a black-powder charge in the center of the warhead is detonated by a timer and the submunitions are expelled in a circular or oval pattern, depending on the range. Each submunition is stabilized by a ribbon parachute as it falls, and explodes on contact.

Tactical Missile System
Tactical Missile System (TACMS)—United States

TACMS can throw a missile some 60 miles.

The Tactical Missile System (TACMS) is designed for deep-interdiction fire missions. It is particularly suited to strike at second-echelon formations such as airfields and reserve troop concentrations. The TACMS launcher carries one missile per pod for a total of two. The missile, which is 13 feet long and two feet in diameter, uses an Arcadene 360 solid rocket motor; four movable tail fins provide maneuvering ability and stabilization in flight. The warhead carries a classified number of M74 anti-personnel/anti-materiel grenades. Range is approximately 60 miles. Information regarding missile weight and the system's overall rate of fire is classified.

TACMS uses the M270 tracked launcher, which has the same chassis as the M2 Bradley Infantry Fighting Vehicle. TACMS carries a crew of three: driver, gunner, and section chief. The launcher weighs 25 tons, is 23 feet long, eight feet high, and 10 feet wide. TACMS can reach a maximum speed of 40 miles per hour and has excellent cross-country capabilities.

Fire control by computer

The guidance system, carried on the M270, consists of a computerized fire control system, an on-board stabilization reference package, a position-determining system, and a built-in rocket pod reloading system. The position-determining system receives signals from Department of Defense navigation satellites to pinpoint its location anywhere in the world. The reloading mechanism enables the crew to draw reloads from a supply vehicle without leaving the armored launcher.

In conditions like those encountered in Kuwait and Iraq, the non-nuclear TACMS gains lethality by dispensing terminally guided submunitions over a wide and open battlefield area.

M-109 (TOW)
M-109 Improved Tube-launched, Optically Tracked, Wire-guided (TOW) Missile—United States

The TOW takes on helicopters and armored vehicles.

The M-109 Improved TOW is a direct descendant of the World War II-era bazooka. Manufactured by Hughes under the designation BGM-71C, the Improved TOW represents a significant enhancement of previous TOW capabilities.

To use, the operator centers the target in the cross hairs of the 13x optical sight. The operator presses the firing button to ignite a rocket motor, which pops the missile from its launch container. To protect the TOW crew from injury, all rocket fuel is consumed before the missile leaves the tube. At a distance of 120 feet, the smokeless sustainer motor ignites and the warhead arms. Before the sustainer motor accelerates the missile to 900 feet per second, four large wings unfold to provide lift. Combustion then stops and the missile glides to its target, with two thin wires trailing behind it.

Standoff probe

The missile is steered by the operator, who watches through the launcher sight and uses a joystick to correct the missile's flight path. A sensor on the launcher watches the flare at the missile's base, computes the angular distance between the flare in the sight and the sight center, and automatically transmits correction signals along the trailing wires. Impact speed at the maximum range of 4,000 yards is greater than 225 miles per hour. The Improved TOW's warhead is fitted with a standoff probe that causes an explosion some 15 inches from the target, which enables it to penetrate heavy armor plate.

The M-109 Improved TOW weighs 57 pounds and is five feet long and six inches in diameter. The original TOW became operational in 1970 with the United States and West German armies. Well over 200,000 TOWs have since been built. In Operation Desert Storm TOW was used as a hand-held weapon, and on armored vehicles and helicopters.

FIM-92A Stinger
FIM-92A Stinger— United States

Few hand-held weapons are ever considered to have a war-winning capability, but the success of the General Dynamics FIM-92 Stinger air-defense system in Afghanistan is widely regarded as primary reason for the Soviet withdrawal from that country.

The Stinger provides portable, one-man antiaircraft fire.

A lightweight system

The Stinger is a one-man, portable, shoulder-launched antiaircraft rocket. The Stinger missile is five-and-a-half feet long, and is launched from a reusable, hand-gripped launcher that contains the Identification, Friend or Foe (IFF) system antenna. The entire system weighs less than 35 pounds.

To fire the Stinger, the operator arms the weapon and clips the IFF unit to his belt; the IFF's electrical cord is attached to the launcher unit. When enemy aircraft appears, the operator lifts the launcher unit to his shoulder and sights the target through an open sight that resembles a three-sided box. The soldier activates the missile's infrared sensor while pointing the launcher at the target. When the sensor has detected and locked onto the enemy aircraft's engine exhaust, the soldier hears a high-pitched, steady tone. The IFF system is used to interrogate the enemy aircraft. If the response is not positive, the soldier pulls the trigger.

The missile is powered by a dual-thrust, solid-fuel rocket motor at Mach 2 speed. Maximum range and altitude are three miles and 15,750 feet, respectively. When in flight, eight control surfaces, four at the nose and four at the tail, "pop up" from the missile's fuselage. The infrared seeker in the missile's nose continues to home in on the target's exhaust plume, providing flight path steering corrections to the missile's guidance command system. The Stinger missile has a hit-to-kill warhead that detonates 6.6 pounds of high explosive to destroy the enemy aircraft.

MIM-104 Patriot
MIM-104 Patriot Tactical Air-Defense Missile System — United States

During its development stage, the MIM-104 Patriot missile system was plagued by cost overruns that nearly resulted in the cancellation of the program. But the Patriot survived, and is now a valuable and successful weapon that has more than proved its worth in combat.

Originally an antiaircraft missile

Designed in the late 1970s as an antiaircraft weapon, the Patriot was modified in the mid-1980s to defend against ballistic missiles as well. The system employs a 17.4-foot-long missile pow-

The Scud-busting Patriot has more than proved its worth.

ered by a single-stage, solid-propellant rocket motor at Mach 3 speeds. The missile weighs 2,200 pounds, and has a range of nearly 43 miles. It is armed with a 200-pound high-explosive warhead that is detonated by a proximity fuse, causing shrapnel to destroy the intended target.

Each Patriot system has eight M-901 storage/transportation containers that serve as launchers, and each launcher has four missiles for a total of 32 missiles. The launchers are attached to the M-860 trailer. The system also has the MSQ-104 engagement control station, which is mounted on an M-818 tractor. The MSQ-104 is a manned unit that uses searching/tracking radar on incoming missiles. A second radar unit, unmanned and trailer-mounted, houses subsidiary ground control radar that is used to search, detect, track, identify, and illuminate the target.

The Track Via Missile (TVM) guidance system is the heart of the system, and accounts for its great accuracy against missiles like the Iraqi Scud, which may be descending at speeds exceeding 3,000 feet per second. The system is so versatile that it can track and steer eight missiles to different targets at the same time.

In the Desert Storm Offensive, the Patriot vs. Scud war has been disparaged as an episode in which the Patriot's dated 1970s technology overcame the even more antiquated 1960s technology of the Scud. And the use of the Patriot over urban areas in Israel occasionally resulted in civilian casualties and collateral damage to buildings from the falling debris of destroyed Scuds. Nevertheless, Patriots managed to rack up a near-miraculous kill ratio against the Scuds, thereby earning the respect of military analysts, as well as the soldiers and civilians it was charged with defending.

SS-1 Scud
SS-1 Scud Short-Range Ballistic Missile System—Iraq

It is a curious fact that a relatively obsolete missile, carrying moderate-sized warheads with imprecise accuracy, has proved to be an important weapon in the Persian Gulf War—at least from a political, if not a military, standpoint.

The Scud has shown itself to be erratic but dangerous.

Intelligence reports vary, but Iraq was supposed to have had as many as 1,000 of the liquid-fueled Scuds prior to the outbreak of the war. Most were intended to be fired from fixed locations, although many were to be launched from mobile platforms as well.

Political and psychological damage

Aside from some minor damage, Scud attacks on Allied bases in Saudi Arabia were rendered ineffective by the U.S. Army's superb Patriot missile. Likewise, the physical damage inflicted on Israeli targets was negligible. But the psychological and political harm they caused was somewhat more significant.

The Scud can trace its history to the mid-1960s, when it began to enter service in the Soviet Union. Scuds were first mounted on tank chassis, then on modern carriers with fair cross-country mobility. The missile was originally designed to carry a 100-kiloton nuclear warhead or a 2,000-pound conventional warhead, with ranges varying from 100 miles to 175 miles, respectively. The principal Iraqi threat lay in the use of Scud warheads containing chemical or biological agents.

The first combat use of the Scud occurred in 1973 during the Arab-Israeli Yom Kippur War; it was later used in indiscriminate attacks against Iranian cities in the Iran-Iraq war of the 1980s. The most dangerous Scuds are the mobile versions, which have a fully amphibious transporter-erector-launcher.

Chemical and Biological Warfare —Iraq

Saddam Hussein has often been compared, usually unfavorably, with Adolf Hitler. During most of

Vigilant defense is maintained against chemical weapons.

World War II the Nazi dictator had at his disposal large quantities of poison gas, and he had studied position papers on the biological warfare option. Yet even at the end, with his world crashing down around him, Hitler never resorted to combat use of either chemical or biological agents. It is quite possible that Hitler, having himself been gassed during the First World War, hated such weapons too much to use them.

Conversely, the Iraqi ruler has demonstrated little restraint where chemical weapons are concerned. On the contrary, he has rarely hesitated to sanction the use of gas when it suited his purposes to do so. At Hussein's orders, the Iraqi armed forces employed gas indiscriminately, and with terrifying effectiveness, against the Kurdish minority within Iraq, and against Iranian military and civilian targets as well.

A tricky proposition

The use of poison gas is an inherently tricky proposition. Nevertheless, prior to the invasion of

Kuwait, Iraq had stockpiled almost 1,500 tons of mustard gas—the terror of the First World War. Mustard gas is a blistering agent; when inhaled, it blisters the lungs, and breathing becomes an agony. More formidable, and deadly, were Iraq's nerve gases—Tabun, Sarin, and VX. A single droplet of nerve gas on exposed skin can cause death within ten minutes.

As Operation Desert Storm got underway, the anticipation of chemical weapons seemed to cause almost as much discomfort and psychological harm as their actual use. Scud missile alerts forced troops to don functional yet cumbersome protective clothing; meanwhile, the civilian population of Israel was held hostage by the threat. Not only were Israeli civilians compelled to keep their gas masks close at hand, they also had to seek refuge in the oppressive sanctuary of sealed rooms. The confused pattern of Scud alarms, both real and false, served to set nerves on end— which may have been Hussein's ultimate goal.

Sea Weaponry

The USS Oliver Hazard Perry *is a guided-missile frigate.*

As Operation Desert Shield/Desert Storm geared up, the United States Navy strengthened its contingent of ships already in the Middle East. Aircraft carriers, battleships, cruisers, destroyers, frigates, and numerous support ships were all deployed to the Persian Gulf, the Red Sea, and the Mediterranean Sea. Since Iraq had a very small and ineffective navy, Allied forces essentially controlled the waves.

The Persian Gulf campaign brought about one event that no expert would have predicted—the reemergence of the battleship as an important element in combat. However, the battleship's 16-inch guns were not the dominant weapon. Instead, the accurate Tomahawk cruise missile—operated against targets considered too dangerous for manned aircraft—proved effective and lethal. Other naval vessels, including cruisers and frigates, also fired Tomahawk missiles, as well as providing escort duty.

Aircraft carriers' fighter jets, attack planes, and other aircraft supplemented the fighting power of Allied air forces. Self-contained, not intruding on the local economy or customs, aircraft carriers proved their worth once and for all.

The sea task force of the United Nations may be a decisive element in an Allied victory, supporting both the air and land forces against Iraq.

Aircraft Carriers
Aircraft Carriers— United States

The aircraft carriers of the United States Navy are the largest and most powerful warships ever built. When at sea, they lead heavily armed squadrons of fighting and support ships in units

The Nimitz *carrier class is represented in the Gulf.*

called battle groups. These mighty ships come in six distinct classes, of which two—*Enterprise* and *Nimitz*—are nuclear-powered. The carriers of the *Midway*, *Forrestal*, *Kitty Hawk*, and *Kennedy* classes are all conventionally powered.

Carrier aircraft attack

The United States Navy perfected the art of carrier warfare during World War II. Since then, U.S. carriers have participated in conflicts ranging from Southeast Asia to Central America, and from the Mediterranean Sea to the Persian Gulf. In Operation Desert Storm, U.S. carrier aircraft struck hard and often at Iraqi military assets. The carriers were also charged with the defense of allied shipping and ground forces.

The Gulf War found the U.S. Navy deploying no fewer than four carriers in the Red Sea: *Saratoga* and *America* (both of the *Forrestal* class), *John F. Kennedy* (*Kennedy* class), and the *Theodore Roosevelt* (*Nimitz* class). On station in the Persian Gulf were the *Midway* (*Midway* class) and the *Ranger* (*Forrestal* class). The *Forrestal* (*Forrestal* class) was dispatched to the eastern Mediterranean to provide air cover for Israel.

The *Nimitz*-class ships are the Navy's largest and most modern aircraft carriers. Each *Nimitz* ship displaces 81,600 tons, has a length of 1,089 feet, a 134-foot beam, and a 38-foot draft. Maximum speed is 30 knots (34.5 miles per hour).

The *Nimitz* ships, like most U.S. aircraft carriers, usually have about 86 aircraft. A typical carrier air wing comprises two fighter squadrons totaling 20 F-14 Tomcats; two strike-fighter squadrons totaling 20 F/A-18 Hornets; two attack squadrons totaling 20 A-6E Intruders; one electronic warfare squadron totaling five EA-6B Prowlers; one airborne early warning squadron totaling five E-2C Hawkeyes; one antisubmarine warfare squadron totaling ten S-3A/B Vikings; and one helicopter antisubmarine warfare squadron totaling six SH-3H Sea King or SH-60F Sea Hawk helicopters.

Battleships
Battleships—United States

Completed in 1943 and 1944, *Iowa*-class battleships were the last ships of their kind to enter Navy service. Moreover, they remain the only battleships in active service with any of the world's navies. As the centerpiece of task forces called surface action groups (SAG), battleships serve as fire support ships and missile-launching platforms for proximate air, sea, and ground operations.

In March 1983, the *New Jersey* became the second ship in the U.S. Navy to receive the Tomahawk cruise missile. Along with the Harpoon antiship missile, Tomahawk land-attack and

*The USS **Missouri** has turned its guns on Iraqi positions.*

antiship missiles now constitute the main armament of *Iowa*-class battleships. The installation of missiles has not come at the expense of traditional heavy guns, however. All *Iowa* ships retain three turrets housing a total of 12 16-guns, with three guns in each turret; and six turrets housing a total of 12 five-inch guns, with two guns in each turret. Additionally, the *Iowa* ships mount four 20 millimeter Phalanx multi-barrel air defense guns.

A new lease on life

In effect, modern missile technology has given the battleship a new lease on life. While not as versatile as aircraft carriers, missile-armed *Iowa*-class battleships are still capable of playing an important role in modern warfare, as events in the Persian Gulf have demonstrated. Many naval experts also contend that the battleships' big guns could, in certain situations, prove more useful than missiles against enemy surface threats and safer and more efficient than aircraft for shore bombardment missions. Indeed, about three weeks into the Desert Storm campaign the *Missouri* used its 16-inch guns in action for the first time since the Korean War, firing them to pound Iraqi bunkers in Kuwait.

The *Iowa*-class battleships displace 57,350 tons, have a length of 887 feet, a 108-foot beam, and a draft of 38 feet. Maximum speed is 33 knots (37.95 miles per hour).

In 1987, the *Missouri* served as part of a multinational task force that was sent into the Persian Gulf to protect merchant shipping during the Iran-Iraq war. The *Missouri* was subsequently joined by the *Wisconsin* prior to the outbreak of hostilities with Iraq in January of 1991. In Operation Desert Storm, the *Missouri* and *Wisconsin* launched Tomahawk missiles at Iraqi targets with extreme accuracy and effectiveness.

Cruisers
Cruisers—United States

Cruisers have long been the naval mainstay of all great maritime powers. They were originally designed to act alone as powerfully armed ships or to lead squadrons of smaller warships. During World War II, U.S. cruisers became the "utility ships" of the Navy, a role that involved them in the majority of ship-to-ship engagements with the enemy.

The 33 cruisers now in service are divided into eight classes; nine of the 33 are nuclear-powered, and the rest are powered by conventional means. Thirteen cruisers are equipped with five-inch

Ticonderoga-*class cruisers carry Aegis radar.*

guns, and ten cruisers have no guns at all except
for 20 millimeter Phalanx multi-barrel air
defense guns.

Antiaircraft escorts

Like the cruisers of yesteryear, these newer
ships serve as antiaircraft escorts for task forces
headed by aircraft carriers or battleships. All are
fitted with surface-to-air missiles and Harpoon
antiship missiles. Some are fitted with Tomahawk land-attack and antiship cruise missiles,
as well as vertical launch missiles like the
ASROC (Antisubmarine Rocket).

Thirteen conventionally powered cruisers are
now under construction. The high cost of nuclear
power plants and related equipment, coupled
with improvements in superpower relations,
make it unlikely that any more nuclear-powered
carriers will be built.

Ten U.S. cruisers participated in Operation
Desert Storm. The most modern ships of this
type belong to the *Ticonderoga* class of conven-

tionally powered cruisers. Equipped with a sophisticated Aegis radar and fire control system and armed with numerous surface-to-air missiles, *Ticonderoga* ships are well suited to carry out their primary mission of task force air defense. Sixteen cruisers in this class are armed with Tomahawk cruise missiles for offensive operations. All *Ticonderoga* ships are also armed with antiship torpedoes and missiles, and two five-inch guns.

The ships of the *Ticonderoga* class displace 9,500 tons, and are 565 feet long, 55 feet in the beam, and have a draft of 32 feet. Maximum speed is 30 knots (34.5 miles per hour). All carry either two LAMPS I Seasprite or two LAMPS III Sea Hawk antisubmarine helicopters.

Destroyers
Destroyers—United States

Ships known as destroyers saw their first major action during the Russo-Japanese War (1904-05). As originally conceived, they were to counter the threat posed to battleships by small, high-speed torpedo boats. In both World War I and World War II destroyers participated in numerous surface engagements against ships of all sizes, and served as general-purpose convoy escorts, antiaircraft ships, and antisubmarine warfare specialists.

Missiles replace guns

Since the end of World War II, the destroyer's weight and armament have changed, and so has

Destroyers of the Spruance *class bristle with armament.*

the definition of its duties. Early on in the postwar era the guided missile proved to be more accurate and more destructive to enemy aircraft than the gun, and it quickly replaced antiaircraft guns as the destroyer's main weapon. Guided missiles were also developed for antisubmarine and antiship warfare, as well as for land-based targets. Today, a missile-armed destroyer can pack the punch of an entire World War II naval task force, even if it isn't armed with nuclear warheads.

The Navy currently has six destroyer classes totaling some 68 ships. About 37 of these are classified as guided-missile destroyers and are armed with large quantities of surface-to-air missiles. While the remaining destroyers also have surface-to-air missiles, their primary concern is antisubmarine warfare. Additional weapons may include antiship missiles and torpedoes, antisubmarine rockets, Phalanx 20 millimeter multi-barrel air defense guns, and five-inch guns.

The *Spruance*-class ships comprise the mainstay of the Navy's destroyer fleet. With their large hulls and block structures, *Spruance* destroyers do not fit the cut-and-thrust greyhound image of the past. Yet they are quite capable, being in fact the most heavily armed destroyers in any navy. The *Spruance* ships even have Tomahawk cruise missiles, which gives them the offensive striking capability of a cruiser or a battleship. The *Spruance* destroyers displace 8,040 tons. They are 529 feet long, 55 feet in the beam, and have a draft of 29 feet. Maximum speed is 32.5 knots (37.4 miles per hour).

Frigates
Frigates—United States

Frigates were originally two-decked sailing ships that carried their armament on the top deck only. Among the more famous of the sail-powered frigates is the *Constitution* (otherwise known as Old Ironsides), which remains a commissioned ship and is berthed in Boston Harbor.

The Oliver Hazard Perry *frigate class has 51 ships.*

The demise of sail-powered warships in the mid- to late-1800s resulted in the disappearance of frigates as well. With the coming of World War II, however, the frigate designation was revived in the U.S. Navy.

The concept of the frigate has remained constant over the years—a small, relatively inexpensive vessel that is swift enough to carry out escort duties. Today, all Navy frigates are anti-submarine warfare escorts. *Oliver Hazard Perry*-class frigates also provide limited anti-air warfare (AAW) protection. The Navy currently has 98 active frigates, with 19 more in the Naval Reserve fleet. The 19 Reserve ships have combined active and reserve crews. No frigates are under construction, and none are planned. Plans to build an advanced-design frigate were canceled in 1986.

Largest ship class

The *Oliver Hazard Perry* class of frigates contains 51 ships, making it the largest single ship class in the U.S. Navy. These ships are armed with torpedoes, surface-to-air and antiship missiles, a 20 millimeter Phalanx multi-barrel air defense gun, and a 75 millimeter rapid-firing cannon. But their two antisubmarine warfare helicopters (housed in twin adjacent hangars located aft on the superstructure) constitute their main armament.

The ships of the *Oliver Hazard Perry* class displace 3,650 tons. They are between 445 and 453 feet long, have a 45-foot beam, and a draft of 25 feet. Like the *Spruance*-class destroyers, *Oliver Hazard Perry* ships are propelled by gas turbine engines that enable them to attain a top speed of 28 knots (32.2 miles per hour).

The U.S. Navy deployed six frigates in the naval component of Operation Desert Storm. As always, they were charged with escort duties for battleship surface action groups, and aircraft carrier battle groups.

Cruise Missiles
Cruise Missiles—United States

The BGM-109 Tomahawk Land Attack Missile (TLAM) was developed by General Dynamics for use by both surface ships and submarines. The TLAM-N has a 200-kiloton nuclear warhead; the TLAM-C and TLAM-D have conventional warheads with 1,000 pounds of high explosives and submunitions, respectively. Another variant is the Tomahawk Antiship Missile (TASM), which is designed for use against surface ships. The

Tomahawk cruise missiles have rocked Iraq.

TASM has a 1,000-pound conventional warhead. All Tomahawk variants are 21 feet long, weigh 3,290 pounds, and have a nine-foot wingspan. Range varies from 285 miles to 1,400 miles.

Unique guidance system

The TLAM uses an inertial guidance system with a unique pattern matching system that compares the features of the surface terrain passing beneath the missile to a map stored in its computer. This enables the TLAM to fly at low altitudes, thus eluding enemy radar detection. The TASM does not have the terrain-following system, which is unnecessary for over-the-water flight. All Tomahawks have a subsonic speed of approximately 500 miles per hour.

The AGM-86B air-launched cruise missile (ALCM) is launched from B-52G and B-52H

Stratofortress bombers, and FB-111 Aardvark bombers. The ALCM is similar in design and performance to the TLAM and TASM series of missiles.

The TLAM and the TASM are fitted on the following ships: *Iowa*-class battleships; cruisers of the *Virginia*, *Long Beach*, and *Ticonderoga* classes; and destroyers of the *Arleigh Burke* and *Spruance* classes. Some of these ships fire their Tomahawks from armored box launchers that serve as storage and launch containers, but most fire the missiles from vertical launchers. Tomahawks can also be fired from 21-inch submarine torpedo tubes and, in the later *Los Angeles*-class attack submarines, from vertical launch tubes.

Literally within the first few minutes of Operation Desert Storm, Tomahawk missiles launched from the battleships *Missouri* and *Wisconsin* struck with astonishing accuracy at Iraqi command centers, radar installations, and other military assets.

Index